Nicholas Whitley

The palæolithic age examined

Nicholas Whitley

The palæolithic age examined

ISBN/EAN: 9783742844910

Manufactured in Europe, USA, Canada, Australia, Japa

Cover: Foto ©Andreas Hilbeck / pixelio.de

Manufactured and distributed by brebook publishing software
(www.brebook.com)

Nicholas Whitley

The palæolithic age examined

THE

PALÆOLITHIC AGE

EXAMINED.

BY

N. WHITLEY, C.E., F.M.S.

HON. SECRETARY OF THE ROYAL INSTITUTION OF CORNWALL,
HON. MEMBER OF THE ROYAL GEOLOGICAL SOCIETY OF CORNWALL.
ETC. ETC.

REPRINTED FROM THE JOURNAL OF THE TRANSACTIONS OF THE VICTORIA INSTITUTE, OR PHILOSOPHICAL SOCIETY OF GREAT BRITAIN.

PREFATORY NOTE.

At an ordinary meeting of the Victoria Institute, or Philosophical Society of Great Britain, specially held at the House of the Society of Arts, the Right Hon. the Earl of HARROWBY, K.G., in the chair ;—

The Minutes of the last meeting having been read and confirmed,

The HONORARY SECRETARY said :—From the great publicity given to the fact that the Institute was about to hold this meeting, to which every leading geologist and palæontologist in the United Kingdom has received a special invitation, it must be apparent that this Society has but one object in view, namely, a full and impartial consideration of the subject.

Mr. W. D. Michell then read a Paper " On the so-called Flint Implements of the Drift ;" illustrated both with numerous diagrams, showing the strata in which the flakes are found, their sizes, shapes, &c. ; and also by his own and three other large collections of flint implements and flint flakes, kindly lent by Professor Tennant, Mr. N. Whitley, and Mr. Borlase.   Mr. J. Evans (now President of the Geological Society) also made a valuable addition to the exhibition by contributing several flint implements.

[It is much to be regretted that Mr. Michell's failing health prevented him from giving more than an imperfect outline of the arguments in his Paper, and even this with much difficulty.   He did not place the MS. from which he read, in the hands of the Society, after the meeting ; hence it cannot be published. ` Mr. Michell never recovered, but died a few weeks afterwards, a martyr to that energy which characterized his life.]

Copies of the following paper by Mr. Whitley were circulated before and at the meeting, and, as in its earlier pages arguments are taken up similar to those enunciated by Mr. Michell, the loss to the Society is less than it would have been had not its author kindly permitted its publication in the Journal of the Institute.

THE PALÆOLITHIC AGE EXAMINED.

INTRODUCTION.

THE most prominent characteristic of the present age is its great intellectual activity and power; and in no other line of thought has this peculiar feature been so fully manifested as in the rapid advance of scientific discovery, and in its practical application to the physical enjoyment and intellectual pleasure of human life : the man of fifty years surveying this progress feels as if he were a Methuselah in the ripe manhood of the gathered knowledge of five hundred years. But the pace is so hard, the competition for leadership so keen, that even in the sober realities of science, the imagination has often run ahead of the judgment; and theories have been built up on the slenderest fragments of unverified facts. To some extent this imperfect perception of the future must of necessity arise from the mode of scientific inquiry, where thought is pushed forward from the known into the dim region of the unknown. It has been notably so in the progress of geological discovery as it passed through all its various phases from the dreams of an Oriental cosmogony into the fixed principles of a noble science, on which it is now so firmly established by the labours of such men as Murchison, Prestwich, and Lyell.

The younger science of anthropology growing into early manhood, in its youthful energy is now rushing into the field with a courage, a power, and a recklessness of theory, as if it were resolved to storm all the garrisons of human thought, and force the dictum of the fiery spirits by whom it is officered on those who do not submit to its sway ; and whom it delights to designate as the "lingering stragglers in the march of science," unable to "carry their vision backwards into the dim past," "and unconscious of the cogency of the evidence on which the great antiquity of man is founded."

This assumption of infallible truth and scornful rejection of all opposing evidence, cannot but clog and retard a branch of scientific inquiry which, if established, must ultimately be built on well-tested and ascertained facts. Science cannot be built on dogmatic assertions ; it cannot rest on a faith which

b 2

relies on authority, but it must have the approval of the judgment to the facts, and the assent of the understanding to the arguments on which it is founded.

I purpose in the following short papers to examine the facts and arguments upon which the Palæolithic age is attempted to be established ; and to give an abstract of the results of antiquarian and geological surveys made to this end, extending in time over a period of ten years, and in range from the Scilly Isles to Norfolk, from Belgium to the Somme, and to Pressigny-le-Grand.

At the outset it is necessary to define the term Palæolithic age, and I am content to abide by the definition of the period given by Sir John Lubbock in his *Pre-Historic Times*, p. 2, in which he describes it as "THAT OF THE DRIFT ; when man shared the possession of Europe with the mammoth, the cave bear, the woolly-haired rhinoceros, and other extinct animals. This we may call the Palæolithic period."

Sir Charles Lyell, writing three years after and describing the Reindeer period of M. Lartet, to which the Caves of the Dordogne belong, says :— "This period may be considered as intermediate between the Neolithic and Palæolithic ages, but it has been classed provisionally by Sir J. Lubbock as Palæolithic." And Sir Charles further manifests a desire to include the cavern deposits in the first Stone age, when he says : —"Lastly we arrive at the still older monuments of the Palæolithic period, properly so called, which consist chiefly of unpolished stone instruments buried in ancient gravels and in the mud and stalagmite of caves." (*Principles of Geology*, vol. ii., 10th ed., p. 559.)

To admit the caverns into the Drift period would be to abandon all that has heretofore been said of the sequence of those deposits. In the description of the Reindeer period, given in *Reliquiæ Aquitanicæ*, p. 25, we read —"Geologically a wide gap separates it from the Drift period." It would also class Neolithic relics and bronze celts* with the Somme tools,—for both of the former are found in caves beneath the stalagmite. I therefore restrict the definition of the Palæolithic ag properly so called, TO THE PERIOD OF THE DRIFT.

The time is now come when this subject can be fully and impartially investigated ; it has been laid before us in great detail in the publications of our leading geologists, and in the journals of the Anthropological Institute ; and time has been given for others to investigate the facts and to gather what to many appears to be conflicting evidence.

In pursuing this investigation I shall examine the facts and weigh the evidence on which the Palæolithic age at present rests, and give the results of my personal surveys of the Drift deposits of England and France, founding my arguments only on well-ascertained natural facts.

The first paper of the series will be on,—

---

* See the description of the Heathery Burn Cave in the *Geologist*, vol. v. p. 167.

5

THE DISTRIBUTION AND ORIGIN OF THE SHATTERED FLINTS AND FLINT FLAKES OF DEVON AND CORNWALL.

The ancient Palæozoic rocks of Devon and Cornwall, elevated and indurated by the eruption of five bosses of granite from Dartmoor to the Land's End, are thrust like a gauntleted fist far out into the Atlantic, unconnected and far removed from any of the secondary formations ; and yet over the high ground of their western extremity, the Rev. John Buller, writing in 1842, mentions that flints are found on the surface of Carn Kenijack, and from thence to Tolpedn-Penwith, over a distance of five miles ; and he suggests that they may have been brought there by the ancient Britons for the purpose of forming out of them arrow-heads, which he says, some of the broken fragments much resemble.* Sir Henry de la Beche, in his geological survey of Cornwall and Devon,† describes the occurrence of flints in the " raised beaches " of the coast-line as " not of easy explanation."

During the past ten years numerous discoveries of apparently isolated nests of shattered flints, chiefly along the northern coast-line, have been made, and many papers have been written on these " *manufactories of flint weapons*," as they have been called ; but further research has shown that these flakes are scattered over a wide area, and that in fact the "nests" form only a portion of a continuous sheet of scattered chalk flints which may be traced over very large portions of the country. This new aspect of the case is best illustrated by one now well-explored district.

Between the village of Croyde and Baggy Point (which forms the northern horn of Barnstaple Bay) the flakes are found abundantly in the subsoil at the mouth of a small transverse valley, and this flint-find was said to be the site of an ancient manufactory of flint implements. But it was soon seen that along the coast section the flints might be traced in the subsoil for at least half a mile ; that on the exposed weather-beaten headland the soil had been weathered off, and there the flints were exposed on the surface ; and even from the arable land of the hill top, especially after heavy rain, the same shattered flints might be gathered from the soil ; and in this way they could be traced eastward through the parishes of Braunton, Heanton, and Pilton, to Barnstaple—a distance of nine miles. Nor was the trail lost there, for eight miles up the valley of the Taw at Bartridge Farm, the flakes were most numerous, and extended from the river up the slope of the hill to at least 200 feet above the valley ; and still further up the Taw, these shattered flints were found at Colleton Barton, to be scattered over an area of 400 acres.

These statements are not founded on any superficial survey of the district, but on discoveries made during a period of many years in carrying out works

---

* *Statistical Account of the Parish of St. Just, in Penwith,* p. 15.
† p. 429.

of drainage, road-cuttings, and sea-embankments; during which time hampers full of shattered flints were brought to me by the workmen, of which about 5 per cent. might be said to be typical flakes and cores more or less perfect, the remainder being crushed flints of undefinable forms. This trail of shattered flints may be roughly estimated to embrace an area of at least 200 square miles of country. It cannot surely be said that a few scattered savages required a manufactory of such a size for the shaping of their stone implements, and therefore it has been sometimes assumed that the widely-scattered flakes are the lost arrow-heads of the Palæolithic hunters; but this fancy vanishes before the consideration that the small proportion of arrow-headed flakes to the larger mass of broken flints is everywhere nearly the same. Continuing the survey of the geographical position of the flakes, we find them scattered over most of the headlands from Morte Point to the Land's End, at Hartland, Budehaven, Stepper Point, and for three miles along the shore of Padstow Harbour, at Trevose Head, Trevalga Island, Newquay Head, the Gannel, St. Agnes, St. Ives, and St. Just. On the south coast of Cornwall the flakes are rare, but they are abundant over a large portion of the table-land of the Lizard Peninsula. But the flakes are not confined to the coast-line: they have been found at three places on the granite plateau of Dartmoor from 1,200 to 1,400 feet above the sea; on barren hills which have never been cultivated between Launceston and Bodmin; by works of drainage on the high lands of Davidstow; on the hills of Constantine; and even on the uncultivated crofts of the Scilly Isles.

If we now compare these roughly-broken flints with the beautifully-formed, barbed, and delicately chipped flint arrow-heads of the Neolithic age, we are at once struck with the lack of evidence which they present of human workmanship. The larger portions are simply crushed and shattered pieces of flint: a diligent search would result in the finding of some rough untrimmed flakes; and from the pick of the mass some thin, well-formed flakes of the arrow-headed type would be obtained, and it is on these alone, to the exclusion of the imperfect specimens, that the assumed evidence of their human manufacture rests. It has been said that the flint flakes and refuse chips of Croyde indicate the site of an ancient manufactory of flint arrow-heads and flake knives. I can discover no evidence in support of such an opinion, but, on the contrary, the evidence that the fractured flints are formed by natural causes appears abundant and conclusive.

1. There is a gradation in form, from the very roughly-fractured flint, so rude that it cannot be ascribed to human workmanship, up to the most perfectly-formed flake of the arrow-headed type.

2. There is a gradation in size, from a flake so minute that it could not possibly be used as a weapon, up to the full-size arrow and javelin heads.

3. The good and the bad are all mingled together in one chaotic mass. This pell-mell mixture of all kinds of flakes and broken flints is perfectly consistent with their being formed by natural causes, but utterly incompatible with their manufacture by man. The most degraded savage would not cast away his perfectly-formed implements with the refuse chips.

4. The flakes are the result of the natural fracture of the flint nodule. I gathered from a heap of flints undesignedly broken for the repair of the roads at Menchecourt, most perfect flint-flake knives, and long, thin, delicately formed "arrow-heads" of the most perfect forms. I have shattered flint-nodules branching in all directions, and all the fractures are longitudinal, and all the points run into the arrow-headed form. I have examined and studied the angular flint gravel of the south of England, the crushed and shattered flints of the Isle of Wight, of the North and South Downs, of the Norfolk drift, and the gravel-pits and surface flints of Belgium and France ; and I find that everywhere the split and shattered flints have a natural tendency to run to the arrow-headed form with sharp cutting edges at the sides.

Their Origin.—It is often put forward as a strong conclusive argument in support of the human workmanship of the flakes, that they are found in places far removed from the natural home of flint in the chalk ; and that they must therefore have been carried to their present sites by man. Thus M. Dupont infers that the flakes in the Belgium caverns were brought from the South of France, and indicate an ancient trade in flint between these countries, ignoring the fact that the flakes are abundant in the soil of Namur, and I have found them near Mons over the Loess in a stratum six inches thick, and scattered by denudation over the surface below. In like manner Sir C. Lyell, writing of the profusion of flakes in the Swiss lake-dwellings, infers that the flint "must have come from a distance, probably from the South of France." (*Antiquity of Man*, p. 20.) Again, the fact is overlooked that a broad band of cretaceous rocks passes along the south of Switzerland at the base of the Alps, and at the head of the valleys whose rivers feed the lakes, from whence these shattered flints and gravel have more probably been swept by denudation into the lakes below. These cretaceous beds are shown on the Geological Map of Europe by Murchison, and more fully in detail by the large Geological Map of Switzerland lately published, which shows that the N.W. shore of the lake of Neuchatel (where the flakes abound, and on which there are twelve lake-settlements) is formed of these flint-bearing beds. The same fanciful origin has been suggested for the flakes found at Croyde, but a more searching and comprehensive knowledge of their geological surroundings leads to a different and more scientific conclusion.

Along the whole coast-line of Devon and Cornwall are found patches of drift of which good sections are exposed by the beat of the waves in the lowlands of sheltered bays, and similar beds cap the cliff in more exposed situations. The bases of these beds contain boulders of foreign rocks which indicate their origin ; at Croyde these drift-beds contain water-worn pebbles and boulders of granite, many varieties of trap, portions of basaltic columns with the angles rounded, and numerous rolled chalk flints ; these drift-beds have been traced south-westward along the whole of the Cornish coast-line. I have further found them on the Scilly Isles, and this trail of flints may be traced over these barren islets to at least 100 feet above the present level of the sea. Following the trail of this drift backwards to its origin, I have found it in South Wales from Tenby to Stackpole Warren, and picked up flint flakes on the summit of Caldy Island. Trimmer has described the well-known white limestone (indurated chalk) of Antrim in the drift of Caermarthenshire.[*] Murchison has marked the flint drift along the western coast of Wales in his geological map; it has left its mark in large characters on the Isle of Man; it has coated the islets and shores of Strangford Lough, and the trail ends with the numerous and often-described "subsoil flakes" of Carrick-fergus and Larne.

On the eastern coast of Ireland we have the evidence of the late Professor Jukes that "chalk flints and pieces of hard Antrim chalk are found in the drift in the counties of Dublin and Wicklow, and along the whole eastern and southern coast of Ireland, at least as far as Ballycotton Bay, on the coast of Cork." (*Manual of Geology*, p. 675.)

The Antrim drift is distinguished by characters which cannot be mistaken: the indurated chalk known as the white limestone, the burnt flints which lie in a bed between the chalk and the basalt, and the basaltic columns themselves, tie up by a threefold cord, which cannot be easily broken, this peculiar drift to its native place in the disrupted chalk of Antrim.

It is important also to observe that these flakes are found in a true geological position, and form a well-defined stratum with other broken stones in the subsoil below the surface-soil: this is so generally acknowledged that they are now known as "subsoil flakes"; and this is not only the case in Ireland and Devon, but it is notably so at Cissbury-hill, at Spiennes near Mons, and at Pressigny le Grand, where they are found by cart-loads, in a stratum two feet below the surface of the soil; thus indicating a geological rather than an antiquarian origin.

In some exposed parts of the Cornish coast "bundles of flakes" are found on the surface: thus, at Trevalga Head the beat of the sea-spray has weathered off the soil, and the exposed flakes and broken pieces of quartz thickly cover the ground, and indicate that the same natural cause which broke the quartz broke the flints.

It is futile to argue against the old surmise that the flints have been brought by vessels in ballast and spread with chalk over the land for manure, for they are now seen embedded in contorted strata of drift in cliff sections, and scattered over infertile crofts, and barren moors which have never been cultivated or manured.

---

[*] "Among the most remarkable of these (fragments) is the hard chalk of the county of Antrim, of which a continuous stream has been traced in Ireland, from its source as far south as Wexford. The tail of this stream of Antrim detritus appears to have caught the Welsh coast, for we have found it in the Boulderclay of the extreme point of Caernarvonshire, and much further to the south, between Newport and St. David's Head, in South Wales." (*Jour. of Royal Agricultural Soc.*, vol. xii. p. 463.)

But it may yet be asked, if these flints were not broken by the hand of man, how were the most perfect of the flakes produced ? This question may not admit at present of a perfectly satisfactory answer. Yet there are well-known forces in nature capable of producing all the phenomena which we have described. The finishing touches of the moulding and carving of our hills and valleys were undoubtedly done by glacial action ; the planing, rasping, and crushing power of a deep mantle of land-ice pushing its tortuous way to the sea, would, on the assumption that a crushed flint occasionally breaks into flakes, produce all the forms of flakes and cores which we find : nor is this a mere assumption, it has been tested by actual experiment. My contractor for the formation of new roads at Eastbourne prepares the metalling by crushing large nodules of flint with " Blake's patent stone-breaker," in which a massive cast-iron jaw is worked by a steam-engine ; the machine breaks the flints as fast as two men can feed it, and from the crushed nodules I have picked out well-formed flakes of all sizes showing the " bulb of percussion " and " wave markings " on the fractured surface, having a conchoidal face on one side and an angular one on the other, and terminating in a bayonet point ; and also " scrapers " and " cores." And these, which cannot be distinguished in form from the so-called implements of the same type of the " Palæolithic age," bear the same proportion to the whole of the mass, as the flakes and cores bear to the rough flints in the various coast-finds.

The evidence which I have brought forward appears to justify the conclusion that the rough, unused, and generally minute flakes are of natural origin ; and I place with confidence these geological facts against the assumption of the fashionable " flint-knife " theory of the day.

Cores, Discs, and Scrapers.

A block of flint showing the loss of flakes from its sides, has been called a core ; and when all the available flakes have been removed " by skilfully-dealt blows," the nucleus is supposed to have been thrown away as useless.

Some of these cores show the loss of one flake only, others of several flakes from one side and a rough shattery fracture on the other side, but the more perfect and typical core is said to have been produced by the flint nodule being first broken transversely, and the flakes afterwards struck off on every side, leaving the core in the form of a small basaltic column.

It is evident that the claim of these cores to be of human workmanship must stand or fall with the human manufacture of the flakes, and the only interest attached to them lies in the evidence which they furnish on this point.

I have lately inspected a gun-flint manufactory at Brandon, and marked the manner in which the flakes are struck off from a block of flint, and the character of the core left and rejected by the flint-knappers. The block is first broken transversely, and in such a manner as to leave a plane surface, and the flakes are then with a heavy hammer struck off by skilfully dealt blows on the edge of the transverse fracture : these flakes are very perfect, with a uniformity of size and shape adapted to the purpose for which they are designed ; they are generally about $3\frac{1}{2}$ inches long, the core being of the same length.

It is obvious to an observer that this uniformity of size and perfection of form is the result of intention and design, and is produced with the greatest ease and certainty. But when we contrast these hand-made products with the subsoil flakes and cores, we find in both these evidences of design wanting. The cores, in particular, are in some instances so minute as to be perfectly useless in producing any implement which could be of use to man ; so minute that they could not have been held in the hand or even between the fingers in order to strike off a flake, as the fingers must have been bruised by the blow rather than the flint ; but this difficulty is met by the assumption, without a tittle of evidence, " that some kind of punch must have been used, instead of the blows being administered directly by a hammer," and it is added, " we have no conclusive evidence for what purpose such minute flakes were used." (*Evans on the Stone Age*, p. 249.)

On the chalk-hills of Yorkshire these small cores abound, and in India, near Jubbulpore, they are found in still greater abundance ; none of these Indian cores exceed two inches in length, more commonly they are from an inch to an inch and a quarter long, and some are not more than half an inch in length. (*Proceedings of the Society of Antiquaries*, vol. iii., n.s., p. 41.) On one of these cores, not larger than an acorn, being half an inch in diameter and three-quarters of an inch in length, are not less than fourteen facets—thus the average size of the flakes struck off would be less than half an inch in length, and about one-tenth of an inch in width ; and even from these small cores smaller flakes must have been produced, as the facets occasionally cross each other, and in some cases at right angles. Is it rational to infer that such minute implements could have been used by man, and that they were in fact so valuable as to have been made with the greatest care and skill with the aid of a punch ? On the other hand, the cores found at Pressigny are from nine to twelve inches long, and so numerous that they may be gathered by cart-loads. Through the courtesy of Dr. Leviellé, of Grand Pressigny, I was shown the shelves of several rooms in his house loaded with such cores, and side by side they bordered the numerous walks of his garden for distances which I could not spare time to inspect.

The subsoil cores are also rude and rugged in the extreme, and the facets are of all sizes, and running in all directions ; in these respects they further differ from those made by the hand of man at Brandon, and the evidence of intention and design is wanting.

But it has been contended that each facet must have been the result of a separate blow ; this is not necessarily the case, for I have cores with from three to five facets on each, formed by one unintellectual blow from Blake's stone-breaker. I discovered near Beachy Head, ten feet deep in drift gravel, and resting immediately on the chalk, a large flint broken *in situ*, and on gently removing it from its bed, I picked out of the shattered pieces two well-formed cores, each having five facets four inches in length. These cores speak for themselves, and confirm the evidence before produced of the natural formation of the flakes.

$\frac{1}{2}$

Discs.—These circular flints are the "sling-stones" of Sir William Wilde and Nilsson, and the "discoidal implements' of Mr. Stevens, who describes them as being nearly circular and coarsely worked, and brought to an edge all round, and considers that they may have been used as missiles. Of these so-called implements the manner of their formation may be readily discovered by common-sense observation of the mode of fracture of the flints on the surface of the ground on the chalk-hills. On a considerable number of surface flints, cup-like cavities are formed on their face perfectly circular in shape, not larger than a sixpence, and often so numerous and close together as to cover the whole of the surface of the flint. In many of these cups the white patina and the discoloration by time is much greater than in others; in some instances it is altogether wanting, and in others the fracture is as fresh as if just broken. Here we have an evidence of age, and an indication that the cups were formed at various and distinct periods of time. The small discs corresponding with the cavities may often be picked up in considerable numbers, and I have found many of them in the ochreous flint gravel which coats the footpaths around Redhill railway-station. The discs also vary in size from that of the smallest button to the largest watch, and some few I have found in the valley of the Little Ouse from four to six inches in diameter, some with the fracture as fresh as if broken yesterday; and the circular cavities or casts from which the discs were dislodged are there also found on the soil, with various depths of patina on their concave surfaces. On Thetford Warren I found what would be described as an ovate implement : it was a simple disc with one diameter somewhat longer than the other, and roughly chipped by being battered on the edges in a *mélée* of gravel, for the wave-markings distinctly indicate that the blows were delivered on the rim, which was thus reduced from a cutting to a blunt edge, and unfitted for any fancied Palæolithic purpose.

It is generally admitted that the "pitting," as it has been called, on flints is due to natural causes, and both Mr. Rose,* F.G.S., and Mr. Hughes,† F.G.S., have attributed these cup-like cavities to the effects of frost ; and Mr. Hughes goes on to show that the naturally chipped flint is so like what he considers the human implement that he cannot distinguish between them. A common-sense view of the many discs of flint found on the soil, and of the perfect cavities from which they were produced, leads irresistibly to the conclusion that they result from natural agency.

It is difficult to understand why Mr. Evans classes discoidal implements with those of the drift,‡ for they are truly surface flints, and are placed by other antiquaries in the Neolithic age.

Scrapers.—These implements, according to Mr. Evans, occur both in the Neolithic and in the Palæolithic age, and are described by him as being of the following forms :—"Horse-shoe Scraper," "Kite Scraper," "Discoidal Scraper," "Oyster-shell Scraper," "Spoon-shaped Scraper," "Duck's-bill Scraper," "Double-ended Scraper," "Hollow Scraper," "Ear-Scraper," "Straight Scraper," "Side Scraper," and "Scraper-like forms." Mr. Evans further says that "Scrapers are very abundant in the French caves . . . and are not wanting in Kent's Cavern and in other British caves. They are, however, of very rare occurrence in the river drift, and when found are hardly ever trimmed to so regular and neatly chipped a segmental edge as those either from the surface or the caves. . . . They appear to have been held in the hand and used in some cases for cutting or chopping, and in others for scraping." (*Stone Implements*, p. 563.) Several of these multiform implements are figured to assist our comprehension ; of one it is said " to have been somewhat worn away by use, whether as a saw or scraping tool it is difficult to say." Another form of "implement" is classed by Mr. Evans as a *scraper*, figured and termed by Sir John Lubbock in his *Pre-Historic Times* as a *knife*, and described by Sir Edward Belcher as a *plane*.§

With great respect I must leave this undefinable form of "implement," this undefined evidence of use, to speak for itself ; the multitude of forms I cannot grasp, the Babel of their tongues I cannot understand. I give it up in despair ; if any man can receive it, let him receive it.

---

* *Proceedings of Geologists' Association*, No. v.
† *Geological Repertory*, vol. ii. p. 128.
‡ *Ancient Stone Implements*, p. 567.   § *Ibid.*, p. 269.

And now let me make an admission to avoid a misconception. It is not my contention that a stone has never been used as a scraper; that a disc has never been hurled as a sling-stone; that a flint flake has never been used as a knife, or never manufactured by man : for both written history and archæological research testify to the contrary. But my contention is, that the shattered flints and simple flakes found in the soil, and more abundantly in the sub-soil, have been formed by natural causes, and unless the so-called implements which have been picked out from the mass of these shattered flints bear other and distinct marks of having been made or used by man, they afford no proof whatever of his workmanship or presence.

I will take an illustration from ancient history. In a journey through the desert of Sinai, the wife of Moses in her haste *took* a "sharp stone" (a flake?) to circumcise her son, and afterwards it is said that Joshua "*made* him sharp knives" (in the margin, knives of flints) for the performance of the same rite ; and at his burial these knives were placed in his tomb. The late geological survey of the Peninsula of Sinai shows a large development of cretaceous rocks near the line of the journey from Sinai to Egypt, where natural flint-flakes are abundantly scattered over the surface of the ground, of which a sample may be seen at the Jermyn-street Museum. Hence it is highly probable that the natural flake was used by Zipporah, and the flake-knife manufactured by order of Joshua.

THE "IMPLEMENTS" OF THE DRIFT.

IT is not too much to assume that there are elements of weakness about the claim of the flakes to be Implements, which lead some of their stoutest defenders at times to express their doubts, and confirm others in absolute disbelief ; and that there is a rebound of opinion from the dogmatic assertion that "a flint-flake is to an antiquary as sure a trace of man as the footprint in the sand was to Robinson Crusoe." Thus, Mr. Hughes, F.G.S., says, "We must allow that flakes with bulbs of percussion, or even flints with faces due to several different blows, are not in *themselves* sufficient evidence of the existence of man."[*] The late Hon. Sec. of the Cambrian Archæological Association has thus recorded his opinion in the Transactions : " I had long ago come to the totally independent opinion that these so-called implements are not made by man, but have resulted from natural operations." Mr. Godwin-Austin, F.G.S., refers to the flakes at the base of the glacial drift of Belgium as being "naturally formed" (*Journal of Geo. Soc.*, Aug. 1866, p. 249); and even Mr. Evans says, " Mere flakes of flint, however analogous to what we know to have been made by human art, can never be accepted as conclusive evidence of the work of man." (*Archæologia*, vol. xxxviii. p. 11.)

But further, the distinction between "High" and "Low-level" gravel,

---

[*] *Geological Repertory*, vol. ii. p. 131.

and the long period of time supposed to have intervened between the deposition of these beds, was shown by myself in 1865 to be founded on imperfect observations, and untenable ;* and in 1868 Mr. Alfred Tylor, F.G.S., in an exhaustive paper on the Amiens Gravel,† has so completely disproved the distinction, that this corps of the defending army has been ordered to the rear.

Thus the outworks are slowly giving way before more detailed investigation, but the citadel on the Somme remains in full strength where the vigilant sentries keep watch and ward. With this fortress Palæolithic man stands or falls. If the "tools" of the Somme type are of human workmanship, then this fortress is placed on an imperishable basis ; but if the assumed evidence of design on the flints will not bear the test of honest criticism founded on diligent research, then this citadel on the Somme must be regarded as an imitation ruin, with which modern landowners fancifully decorate their parks, and is distinguished by the name of a "Folly."

The simple issue to be tried is, as Sir John Lubbock clearly puts it, " Are the so-called flint implements of human workmanship ?" and this proposition, which Sir John undertakes to prove (*Pre-Historic Times*, p. 276), he does not support by a tittle of evidence, but he does prove convincingly that the flints are found in undisturbed gravel; that they have marks of age on their surfaces by which the genuine implements can be known from forgeries ; and then Sir John assumes that he has proved his case, and says, "On this point, therefore, no evidence could be more conclusive."

This is a mistake of the question. *It is proved* that the flint is found deep in the gravel-beds, which no one who has inspected the beds can doubt ; but it is *not proved* that the flint has been formed into an implement by man. The zeal of the antiquary has in this argument clouded the judgment of the scholar. It must also be stated that the accomplished geologist, Sir C. Lyell, has fallen into the same argumentative mistake ; he says, "As much doubt has been cast on the question whether the so-called flint hatchets have really been shaped by the hands of man, it will be desirable to begin by satisfying the reader's mind on that point." (*Ant. of Man*, 1st ed., p. 112.) But in the following pages this vital point is not discussed, and no evidence whatever in reference to it is given ; " the genuineness of the implement " is inferred from the " vitreous gloss," the dendritic markings which only indicate age are figured, and the subject is closed by a quotation from Professor Ramsay, who had written : " For more than twenty years, like others of my craft, I have daily handled stones, whether fashioned by nature or art ; and the flint hatchets of Amiens and Abbeville seem to me as clearly works of art as any Sheffield whittle."

I will put quotation against quotation. " Wherever," says Hallam, " obsequious reverence is substituted for bold inquiry, truth, if she is not already

* *Flint Implements from Drift not Authentic*, p. 31.
† *Journal of Geological Soc.*, vol. xxiv. p. 103.

at hand, will never be attained." If the two inquirers above named have thus failed in their logic, there is at least some foundation for the words of Dr. Carpenter, that "no logical proof can be adduced that the peculiar shapes of these flints were given to them by human hands." The leading advocates for the "Implements" have failed on this point of their case. I will now show cause against the human manufacture of the so-called tools. My arguments naturally divide themselves into two parts—the evidence from the flints themselves, and the collateral evidence of their surroundings ; and in this inquiry I shall follow the sound canon of scientific criticism, of judging the unknown by the known.

Let the flints speak.

1st. *The Palæolithic implements are all of flint,* and in this respect they differ from the recognized stone tools of the Neolithic age, which are not only made of flint, but also of " serpentine, greenstone, granular-greenstone, indurated claystone, trap, quartz, syenite, schistus, yellow hornstone or chert, granular porphyry, siliceous schist, serpentine or jade." (*Jour. of Brit. Arch. Assoc.,* vol. iii. p. 127.) Professor Nilsson has put this fact forward in still greater detail, and adds, " From all this we come to the conclusion that in Scandinavia, as in the South- Sea Islands, the savage did not confine himself to one single material for his implements, but had resort to any suitable substance that he could obtain." (*The Stone Age,* p. 101.) But it seems that Palæolithic man would not allow himself any choice of material— he would have flint or no hatchet ; but this is contrary to all we know of the usages of savages, of which a good illustration may be taken from the implements found in the north of Ireland, where flint is naturally broken into knives and arrow-heads ; but even here, we learn from the catalogue of the Museum of the Royal Irish Academy, that the majority of the Neolithic implements were made of greenstone, basalt, trap, and hornblende rock. I put this known fact of what man really did, against the fancy of what he was supposed to do.

2nd. *The " implements" are all of one type.* —This does not refer to size, for the " hatchets" vary in length from two to ten inches ; nor to finish, for many of them are very roughly chipped ; but to a characteristic identity of form which pervades these chipped flints. Mr. Flower considers that there are fifteen or sixteen distinct types ; Mr. Evans divides them into eight varieties, all duly named, and then adds, " I am far more ready to think that only two main divisions can be established, though even these may be said to shade off into each other." But, though of all sizes and various forms, they constitute a type totally and entirely distinct from **any** known imple- ments ever used by man. This of course raises a **strong** presumptive evidence against their being implements at all.

But this type is so distinct, and the implements, wherever found, bear its impress so completely, that it has been inferred that savage man made them by instinct, as the bird builds its nest, and the bee its cell : there is, however, a more rational interpretation of this universal similarity of type. The tools made by man to supply his wants show great variations of constructive ingenuity. In the Museum of the Royal Irish Academy there are no less than 688 bronze celts, and they all vary in make, and Sir J. Lubbock says, "Moreover it is a very remarkable fact, especially when we consider the great, I might say the immense, number of bronze celts which are found, that scarcely two of them have been cast in the same mould. (*Prehistoric Times*, p. 166.) On the contrary, crystalline rocks break by nature into the same forms wherever found : thus the similarity of type in the drift flints is not a characteristic of the work of man, but it is of the work of nature.

3rd. *The Drift implements show no marks of having been used by man.*— It is supposed that some of these implements were used as weapons both of war and the chase, others to grub up roots, to cut down trees, to scoop out canoes, to cut holes in the ice, as wedges for splitting wood, and for grubbing and tilling the ground ; in fact, as savages using stone implements in any age must have used them to supply their wants, the evidence of use impressed on the flints must therefore have been of much the same character in all ages.

The cutting edge of the flakes generally shows the natural serrated fracture of the flint, and only in one instance have I found a flake ground into a chisel-like form at the end and polished by use ; this was, however, a surface implement.

On the soil at the west of Menchecourt village, I found a flint celt of the true Stone age ; it had been ground into form, but the point was worn back by use, and on it was a long polished cavity about the size of a quill, as if it had been much used in rubbing a strip of leather into a rounded thong.

After a detailed review of the Scandinavian tools, Nilsson says, " These facts show that the above-mentioned stone objects have been employed as tools in everyday use, and that they have, while being so used, become worn, resharpened, and broken, and that the fragments have been made into other kinds of tools." (*The Stone Age*, p. 90.)

Most of the drift " tools," on the contrary, have their edges so sharp that they show no marks of use, and it is then inferred that there must have been a manufactory on the spot. Others have their edges worn by being rolled in a river's bed, or battered by the mass of gravel in which they are found. I obtained from the gravel-pits of the Somme thirty " implements," and in no case were the edges ground or polished, or bore any marks of having been used for any purpose whatever ; where the point was sharp from fracture, the edges at the sides were equally sharp from the same cause, and some of the specimens, partly rounded by being rolled in water, had their edges worn precisely to the same extent as the points, and the edges of all the split contiguous flints presented the same appearance.

I have inspected a very large number of the Drift " tools," perhaps 1,000, and I say advisedly, that I have not seen one bearing the same indubitable marks of use as characterize the true stone implements of the Neolithic age, nor do I find in any of the various scientific journals mention made of any such evidence of use. Sir Charles Lyell does indeed venture to suggest that the rounded angles of some of the implements may have been occasioned by use, but he qualifies his language in a manner due to his high position when he says, "Out of more than 100 flint instruments which I obtained at St. Acheul, not a few had their edges more or less fractured or worn, either by use as instruments before they were buried in the gravel, *or by being rolled in the river's bed.*" (*Antiquity of Man.* p. 113.) And Mr. Evans expresses his doubts in much the same manner on the individual specimens ; of one he says, "its angles are slightly waterworn, and the edges worn away, either by friction among other stones in the gravel, *or by use*" (*Stone Implements*, p. 485) ; and of others, "They bear evident marks of abrasion and bruising at the ends, such as may have resulted from their use as hammerstones" (p. 489) ; and again, "Many appear to have their edges chipped by use" (p. 526). And on such dubious marks of use, we find in his recent work the oft-reiterated assertion, that the Drift implements show marks of wear. It is a sufficient answer to this sort of evidence to reply that the roughly fractured gravel in which these symmetrical chipped flints are embedded, bears the same marks of wear, of bruising, and chipping, as are found on the assumed implements.

The so-called worked flints of Pressigny are so abundant that they impede the cultivation of the land ; they abound in the soil in every direction, and the concurrent testimony of many observers is, that notwithstanding their wonderful abundance, they show no marks of having been used by man.*

4. *Their Number.*—Of the flint tools at Hoxne, Mr. Frere said, "The number of them was so great that the man who carried on the brick-field told me that before he was aware of their being objects of curiosity, he had emptied basketfuls of them into the ruts of the adjoining road." At the newly discovered finds on the Little Ouse, hundreds are procured from a single gravel-pit, and these pits dot the sides of the valley for eight or ten miles. At Abbeville, M. de Perthes writes, "Any one visiting me may count them by thousands, and yet I have kept only those which presented some interest. From those beds which I have called "Celtic," I have seen them drawn in barrows to metal the neighbouring roads—one would have thought a shower of them had fallen from the sky." At St. Acheul, in about three acres of land, certainly more than 3,000 tools have been exhumed, which is equal to 640,000 in a square mile, and as these beds are now proved to extend more than twenty square miles along the valley of the Somme, if equally productive, there must be 12,800,000 in this small area ; the present population of France is less than 200 to a square mile, and these implements are assumed to have been lost by a race of hunters, when from the nature of their pursuits the country could have sustained only a very sparse population. It has been calculated that 800 acres of hunting-ground produce only as much food as half an acre of arable land, and on this

---

* Mr. Evans says, "At Pressigny, so far as I could see, the large *livres de beurre* show no sign of use or wear." (*Brit. Association*, 1865.)

c

basis *the ratio of lost axes to the savage population would be as six millions to one.*

I have thus given in a condensed form the evidence of the flints themselves ; it remains to produce the testimony of their belongings.

The Drift "Implements,"—their Surroundings.

If we should happen to find on the surface of a chalk down a rough flint which appeared to have been used as a strike-light, the evidence of its association with man at best would be but dubious and uncertain ; if we ound the same rough flint in a kist-vaen, the probability would be much greater that such had been its use ; but if we found it in a hut-circle, carefully placed with other recognised tools of man, then there would be the highest probability that the flint had been used as an implement to minister to man's wants.

From this point of view, what is the nature and value of the evidence deducible from the surroundings of the Drift "implements,"—does it indicate their artificial character, or does it testify to their natural formation ? This is the case we now have to try.

1. *Both the flakes and the "implements" are in a section, found in true geological stratum.*—In Cornwall and Devon, at the base of the soil, and mixed with the top of the more clayey subsoil, there is generally found a thin layer of angular crushed stones, not strictly related to the rock below, but derived in part from it, and in part drifted ; and this is more especially the case where veins of quartz abound, for here the general denudation of the country has carried away the softer materials, but the hard crystalline quartz has resisted the abrasion, and has been left scattered over the then surface of the ground before the true soil was deposited ; which is, as Mr. Trimmer correctly describes it, "the warp of the Drift." The crushed quartz is especially plentiful on the barren hills of Cornwall, and in reclaiming this down-land the Cornish farmer trenches it deeply, digs out the "cold spar," and piles it up by the roads and fences, in the same manner as the French cultivator at Pressigny carts off the flakes and cores. The subsoil flakes occupy the same geological position as this broken quartz, and indeed they both are often mixed together in the same bed, and this pell-mell mixture of the crushed fragments is very observable on the projecting headlands on the north coast of Cornwall. At Trevalga Head, the powerful beat of the Atlantic spray has weathered off the thin soil and left the pieces of quartz and the flakes of flint mingled in one mass on the surface. On the inland rugged granite moors, up to the time of the introduction of lucifer-matches, the Cornish tinner was in the habit of picking out of the subsoil the flint flakes as strike-lights for his pipe. I will only further mention that at Cissbury Hill, Pressigny le Grand, and Spiennes, the flakes lie in a thicker stratum, and their geological belongings are yet more obvious.

Turning now to the so-called axes of the Somme type, we find their geological horizon in the Drift most clearly defined in the sections of the gravel-pits at St. Acheul; there the "implements" lie at the bottom of the bed, mingled with angular flint gravel, the whole having a general uniformity of size, conformable with their geological deposition. It is obvious at a glance, that the angular gravel and the implements must be referred to the same common origin : they are similar in their nature, in the colour and depth of the patina, in the amount of wear from being rolled in water, and in the character of the chipping on their faces; and all their antecedents are geological, and not antiquarian; and the unquestionable inference is, that they were lodged in the gravel by natural causes, perfectly irrespective of the will of man. It is, in fact, so obvious that they must have had a geological origin, that to bridge over the difficulty it has been surmised (and on this subject there is no end of surmising) that the "implements" have been swept away from ancient Palæolithic villages by land floods, and deposited in their present geological position. This fancy, no doubt, evades the full force of the geological argument, but it places the evidence of the origin of the " implements" beyond the reach of scientific inquiry, and builds the Palæolithic age on an invisible foundation, which I need not attempt to overthrow.

Again, it has been surmised that, from the great abundance of the "implements," there must have been a manufacture of them on the spot. Of this we know nothing—the proof lies beyond human ken and scientific research, —but this we do know, that whoever built the supposed manufactory, the storehouse in which they were lodged was undoubtedly built by the hand of Nature.

2. *Their geographical distribution.*—The home of the entire flint nodule is in the upper chalk, and the home of the so-called implement is in the angular flint-gravel and flint-drift; their paternity is geological, and this relationship is so close and intimate that it has never been broken. Thus the flakes of the north of Ireland adhere closely (except where drifted) to the green ribbon indicating the chalk, and which encircles on the geological map the basalt of Antrim. The instructive geological map of Europe, by Sir Roderick Murchison, shows us that the Somme drains a large *cretaceous* district, that Hoxne, Bury St. Edmund's, and Brandon, are in the middle of a *chalk* plateau, that the beach at Herne Bay and the Reculvers is bounded by a *chalk* cliff, that Fimber is in the middle of the *chalk* district of Yorkshire, that Fisherton is at the foot of the *chalk* plain of Salisbury; and it is well known that all the valley gravels in which the "implements" have been found, are mainly composed of *flint detritus*. Nor can we stop here; the caverns of the Dordogne, of Sicily, and the site of the flint flakes from Syria and Arabia Petræa, are all intimately connected with *cretaceous* formations. This connection of the geographical distribution of the implements with geological structure has been pointed out in greater detail by the Treasurer of the Anthropological Institute, Mr. Flower, who says : " It is a remarkable circumstance, in relation to these deposits, that they occur only within a comparatively limited area. No true Drift implement has, I believe, ever been found in countries lying north of Great Britain; nor in

Great Britain have they been found to the north-west of a line drawn from the Severn to the Wash in Norfolk—a distance of two hundred miles, and in the direct line of the Lias escarpment ;" and he further adds the suggestive fact, " It is worthy of remark that the line of demarcation between the Drift-implement districts and those destitute of them, nearly corresponds with the line which divides the boulder-clay districts from those destitute of boulder-clay. (*Jour. of Anthrop. Inst.*, Jan. 1872, p. 284.)

On the other hand, *far from the chalk*, on the ancient rocks of Norway and Sweden, there are no Palæolithic tools ; the Museum of " Copenhagen contains more than 10,000 polished stone axes and other implements of stone, and that of Stockholm not fewer than 15,000 "; " but the Palæolithic types are absolutely unknown there."* The same kind of evidence is yet more conclusively derived from the ancient valley gravels of Cornwall ; these stanniferous gravel-beds have been thoroughly explored through at least a period of 2,000 years, in search of the " stream-tin " which they contain, and yet not one " tool " of the true Drift type has ever been found in them. Is it conceivable that Palæolithic man selected only as his dwelling-place the dry and thirsty lands of the chalk-wolds, where no water is ; that he so loved the bare and barren sands which now constitute the rabbit warrens of West Norfolk, as to leave his weapons there by thousands ; and that he abhorred to dwell in the rich valleys of the new red sandstone, or in the " golden valleys " at the foot of the Oolite escarpment, where no such relics of his presence can now be found ; or is it not more rational to infer that this close relationship of the geographical distribution of the " implements " to geological structure is the result alone of natural causes ?

3. *No relics of man are found in the Drift with the so-called Implements.*— Wherever man has been known to have existed, even in his most degraded state, there the evidences of his former presence are multiform. The people of the ancient lake-dwellings of Switzerland, in addition to their stone implements, left behind them the relics of their pottery, their food, their raiment, their ornaments, their habitations, and indications of their habits and pursuits ; but when we turn from these abundant evidences of man's presence, to the consideration of the evidence presented by the Drift beds, we find roughly-chipped flints, and these alone ; not a bone of man's frame, not a shred of his clothing, not a fragment of his pottery, not a trace of his habitation, or any indication of his works or pursuits : nothing but roughly-chipped flints dignified by the name of axes, and unlike in form and type any implements ever known to have been used by man ; and this form passes by such insensible gradations into the other forms of the rough angular gravel in which they are embedded, that the assumed evidence of design becomes obscured and obliterated. In the whole history of inductive science it would be difficult again to find a case in which so large a superstructure was attempted to be built on so slender a foundation.

----

* Sir John Lubbock's *Introduction to Nilsson's Stone Age*, p. xxiv.

It may, however, be said that other relics of man have been found ; that there is tho testimony of the human jaw discovered by Boucher de Perthes deep in the Abbeville gravel.   I need not stay to expose this fraud : all the scientific evidence is against the antiquity of the bone ; it has been abandoned as an unreliable relic by those who have examined the facts ; and it is now only held to by a few enthusiastic antiquaries with that fantastic faith—

"which once made fast
To some dear falsehood, hugs it to the last."

But there is the more important statement, supported by the authority of a few great names, that in the gravel-pits of St. Acheul, the beads which formed the necklaces of these ancient people have been discovered. From this spot I obtained seventy-two specimens of these so-called " beads "; some of them had slight indentations on their surfaces, in others the perforations extended much deeper, and the more perfect specimens had a hole completely through their centre ; these, when arranged according to their sizes, and placed on a string, form a very imposing supposititious necklace. The aid of science has been called in to determine the origin of these subglobular perforated bodies : they have been examined by Professor Rupert Jones and Dr. Carpenter, and pronounced by them to be fossil organisms of the chalk. Professor Jones expresses such a clear and decided opinion as to their origin, that it puts an end to all controversy ; he says they " occur in Bedfordshire, and at St. Acheul ; I have to state that, as everybody knows, they have been derived from the chalk, in which similar fossils are abundantly found, either in the perforated condition, or solid, or with a more or less shallow hole in their substance. . . . The concavity of the typical variety becomes in many of the globular forms a small cavity, a hole, or even a neat cylindrical perforation. The last feature may be due, perhaps, to the *Orbitolina* having grown around a smooth stem of seaweed. At all events *such perforated specimens are natural*, and as abundant in the chalk as those of different conformations. . . . I may add that the imperforate *Orbitolinæ* occur in the gravels just as much as the perforate. Also that the perforation of the non-drifted *specimens in the chalk* is often just as smooth and straight as if artificial ; the interior surface is not worn, however, but consists of a natural structure of the organism." (*The Geologist*, vol. v. p. 235.)

Thus these so-called beads are undoubtedly natural products, and they afford no proof whatever of the early existence of man ; they must be classed with such relics as St. Hilda's snakes, St. Patrick's loaves, and St. Cuthbert's beads ; and to arrange them on a string in the form of a necklace, and dangle them before the eyes of the uninformed as a relic and ornament of Palæolithic man, is to drag science back into the ignorance and superstition of the dark ages. It is impossible for any scientific man to recognize in these globular fossils the evidence of human manufacture.

Thus we arrive at the conclusion that all the surroundings of the "impelments" testify to their natural production, and that their origin is geological and not antiquarian.

I have now brought this examination to a close, having endeavoured to present the evidence which has determined my own opinion in as clear a light, and in as fair a manner as possible. It cannot be thrust aside or ignored as irrelevant. It is not answered by the reiterated cry that "the flint hatchets of Amiens and Abbeville are as clearly works of art as any Sheffield whittle." It is in vain for author after author to write whole pages to prove the "authenticity" and "genuineness" of the "implements," when such misleading words are found only to refer to the discovery of the flint in the gravel, and not to the human manufacture of the tool. I have shown by the evidence of the flints themselves, and by their relationship to the surrounding gravel, that their origin is natural, and not artificial.

> "To the solid ground
> Of nature trusts the mind which builds for aye."

At the conclusion of Mr. Michell's paper,

The CHAIRMAN said,—It is now my duty to move a vote of thanks to Mr. Michell for his paper, and to mention that any here are at liberty to join in the debate thereon ; as there are some present whom we are specially anxious to hear, may I to call on Mr. John Evans kindly to commence the discussion.*

Mr. J. EVANS, F.R.S.—I am sure that all present sympathize with the author of the paper, and regret the indisposition which has prevented him from laying his views before us with as much facility as he would otherwise have done. I will preface what I have to say with the remark that he and I, as well as a good many of those who are well acquainted with the manufacture of flint instruments in modern times, and who have studied the question of their production in ancient times, hold very different views. Mr. Michell has attempted to show that instead of these implements (for such, with all respect for him, I must still continue to call them) being of human manufacture, their forms and appearances are due to some mysterious natural causes. In the first place, he has taken up the question with regard to the flint flakes, some of which lie upon the table,—simple forms of flint which are made, at the most, with two or three blows,—upon the evidence furnished by which, when they are found in gravel, unless they occur in considerable numbers, and bear upon their edges the signs of having been used, I am not aware that any archæologist has ever attempted to rely. The bulk of the flakes to which the author of the paper alludes—I mean those which

---

* With a view to carrying out the main object of the Institute, in holding a meeting to which all who take any side in the Flint implement controversy were invited to come and to speak freely, the Editor has forborne to make any correction or curtailment in the following speeches.—[ED.]

are found in such abundance all over the western portion and the centre of England, as well as through almost every other country—have nothing to do with the Palæolithic age, but in reality belong to the Neolithic period down to the time of the Romans, and even more modern dates. Flint is one of those indestructible bodies which when once chipped into form, unless subsequently broken, retains the shape into which it was fashioned, and you may consequently find flints retaining at the present day the same form they possessed almost any number of years ago. When we consider the number of years during which all of us will acknowledge this country has been inhabited, and that for the purpose of producing fire, flint has been in use nearly the whole of that time ;* and if we then take a population of a thousand for two or three square miles of country, and assume that for fire-making purposes only one flint was chipped by each person in a year, and that that flint produced 20 splinters, you would thus have 20,000 flakes, and if you put the occupation of the country at 2,000 years, you would in that way have 40,000,000 flakes, or, as I would call them, the "strike-a-lights" of our ancestors. This, I say, is the reason why so many flints are found showing signs of blows upon them in the shape of that bulb of percussion which the author of the paper contends does not give evidence of human manufacture. This bulb of percussion occurs where the splinter or flake of flint is dislodged from another piece of flint by means of a blow. The flint is to a certain extent compressible, and where the blow is administered, the body of the flake is driven slightly inwards, and the fracture being prolonged, produces either a cone or the section of a cone. You may in this way produce a beautiful conical surface on a flint, the cone extending into the body of the flint sometimes as much as an inch. This brings me to the other objections that have been raised by the author of the paper ; and here I may say that inasmuch as the paper which has been written by Mr. Whitley

---

* Flint was in use, even up to the year 1841, in the metropolis of this country. The mode of producing fire adopted in the present day in Africa, Australia, the Pacific Islands, and indeed in all uncivilized countries, is by drilling or rubbing pieces of wood together ; and if we may argue in the usual way, from the present to the past, the earlier inhabitants of this country must have produced fire in a similar manner, indeed history goes far to tell us so. With regard to the next portion of Mr. Evans's ingenious theory, there is no record of any country ever having possessed a population at the rate of 500 to the square mile. The present population of the United Kingdom is 292, of France, 200 to the square mile. The population of England and Wales has greatly increased of late ; in 1871, it was twenty-two and three-quarter millions (or at the rate of 389 to the square mile) ; in 1801 it was nine millions ; and in 1550, four millions. The origin of the flint flakes of the Drift has been alluded to by many ; one writer has found a reason for the existence of the "strike-a-lights" of Mr. Evans, in the action of the ice and boulders in the glacial age, action which must have been very similar to that produced by Blake's stone-crusher, specimens of the flakes formed by which were produced at the meeting : these had many of the peculiarities alluded to by Mr. Evans as having been caused by a blow.—[ED.]

on this subject has been placed in the hands of nearly everybody present, and as Mr. Michell seems to have adopted almost entirely Mr. Whitley's views ; I will take the four points Mr. Whitley has raised against the artificial origin of these Palæolithic implements. I will put, for the moment, these imperfect flakes entirely out of the question, and at once deal with Mr. Whitley's objections. He states, in the first place, that the Palæolithic implements are all of flint, and I believe he infers that the fractures upon them are all the result of a natural agency acting on some property belonging to the flint. When I say that it is not the case that all these Palæolithic implements are of flint, but that they are found chipped out of other materials, and yet that they are still of analogous forms to those which are made of flint, the argument that they are attributable to the natural fracture of flint from ordinary causes must, I think, fall to the ground. I have here two specimens that are almost identical in form and size, and that are chipped in the same manner ; but one of them is of flint, while the other is of felsite, or greenstone.* One of them was found at St. Acheul, and the other in the neighbourhood of Brandon. I have also an implement of quartzite from the Madras Presidency, as well as other implements made of three different materials, each breaking in a different manner, but all wrought into analogous forms, and consequently evidencing that they must be the result of human workmanship. In the second place, I am told that the implements are all of one type, and that therefore they must be due to natural causes.† I cannot imagine on what grounds Mr. Whitley makes such an assertion as this, for to maintain that the two implements I have here are of one type might, I think, be fairly characterized as a monstrous perversion of terms. Mr. Michell, indeed, goes so far as to acknowledge that there are two types, and others are able to carry them further ; but no doubt there is a gradation observable between one type and another, and this fact, to my mind, is sufficient to show that they are the result of workmanship applied in a certain direction, sometimes forming an oval cutting tool, and sometimes a sharp cutting instrument of a different shape, each being applied to a different purpose. So much, then, with regard to the implements being all of one type. Here is another form of implement with a cutting edge at the side (producing it), and here is a large broad flake with a simple face on one side, showing the cone, or bulb of percussion, while the other side shows the results of a series of blows, each of them producing a separate facet. Then, again, Mr. Whitley

---

* The implements produced by Mr. Evans were of the Neolithic period. Mr. Michell (whom I questioned), and every one in the room recognized them as beautiful specimens of workmanship, totally different in character from the *flakes*, the subject of Mr. Whitley's and Mr. Michell's paper. Mr. Evans, and especially Dr. Carpenter, seem to have considered that Mr. Michell desired to class such implements with the flint flakes of the Drift, in which they were entirely mistaken, and it is to be regretted that Mr. Michell did not correct this misapprehension.—[Ed.]

† This remark appears to have been made by Mr. Whitley with regard to the *flakes*.—[Ed.]

says that the flint implements which have been found, show no marks of having been used by man. Now, Mr. Whitley has done me the honour to quote my book on one or two occasions, but if he had looked into it a little further than he appears to have done, he would have seen instance after instance in which there are distinct marks of these implements having been worn by use on the edges. I state that in nearly all the implements of one particular type there are, on the side of the bulb, marks where the implements have been used for the cutting or scraping some hard substance, and if you will take a newly-wrought flint and use it to scrape bone, you will produce upon it precisely similar marks of wear to those which you see here (showing a specimen). In nearly all the cases in which the implements are discovered in beds of clay or sand, instead of being found in the gravel, in the transport of which their edges are rolled by the action of the surrounding stones, so that it is difficult to trace the signs of actual wear, it is rather the exception than the rule that you should find on their edges no marks of wear. This, to my mind, is a strong argument in favour of the conclusion that they must have been of human origin; for you could hardly say that the men who existed in those early times would have been able to select a sufficient number of implements naturally formed. Nor can we suppose that the same natural causes which might lead to the fracture of flints in this peculiar way, when embedded among other hard substances, such as gravel, would lead to their being fractured in precisely the same manner when embedded in clay, especially where no splinters are found near them. Another argument used by Mr. Whitley is that the implements are found in such great numbers. As I have already explained, the wonder is not so much that they are found in such large numbers, but that we do not find more of them. But let us take the case on this ground alone. What does it prove? Why that they must of necessity be of artificial origin, because it is only in gravels of a certain position and age, and associated with a certain description of fauna, which is now for the most part extinct, that these implements are found. (Hear.) If you search in gravel of an analogous character, but belonging to a different age, you find no implements. As I understand Mr. Michell, he holds that in most cases these implements are stained in a similar manner to the stones in the gravel among which they are found, and is willing to accept the assumption that if they are of human origin they are of the same age as the gravel itself. The question, therefore, is, what is the real age of the gravel itself? This is a question, however, into which I will not now enter, as I have already entered into it elsewhere.* But I will point out that in some cases these implements,

---

* Dr. Dawson, in his *Earth and Man*, propounds the theory, that at the close of the glacial period, the land rose slowly out of the waters, the clay deposits of the glacial waters being marked over and rearranged by the waves. As the land rose further, its surface was modified by violent rains and streams, by which the valleys were ploughed, plains levelled and overspread by alluvium; and thus it is difficult to discriminate between the river alluvium of

instead of being of the same colour as the gravels in which they are found, are of a different colour altogether, showing that they have previously been deposited in certain beds where they have obtained the colours they exhibit, and that they have afterwards been transported to, and deposited in the beds in which we now find them. I have here a few specimens of the implements of the Neolithic (or Later Stone) period, in which age the hatchets were frequently ground so as to form a cutting edge ; but in the case of implements from the gravel, we have not discovered any which bear signs of grinding upon them.[*] I am quite prepared to accept what Mr. Michell has

---

this age and the deposits of the sea, or the older glacial beds ; and to distinguish fossils of the older post-pliocene, which must often, in the process of sorting by water, have got mixed with those of the newer. After animal and vegetable life had overspread the new land, palæolithic man was introduced, on the Eastern Continent, and was contemporary with both existing and extinct species. Dr. Dawson adds, " in thus writing, I assume the accuracy of the inferences from the occurrence of worked stones with the bones of post-glacial animals. After this there seems to have had a rapid subsidence and re-elevation of the earth, the geological deluge, which separates the post-glacial from the modern, and the earlier from the later prehistoric period of the archæologists ; and it is 'not impossible that this constituted the deluge of the Bible. As to the time required for the post-glacial period it has been much exaggerated, the calculations of long time based on the gravels of the Somme, the cavern deposits, the delta of the Tinière, and the peat bogs of France (the peat bog of Abbeville is a forest peat, and the stems in it show that it grew at the rate of three feet in a century ; it is 26 feet thick), and Denmark, on certain cave deposits, have all been proved to be at fault, and probably none of these reach further back than 6,000 or 7,000 years, which, according to Dr. Andrews (*Transactions of the Chicago Academy*, 1871), have elapsed since the close of the boulder-clay deposits in America. In 1865 I had an opportunity of examining the now celebrated gravels of St. Achenl, on the Somme, by some supposed to go back to a very ancient period. With the papers of Prestwich and other able observers in my hand, I could conclude merely that the undisturbed gravels were older than the Roman period, but how much older only detailed topographical surveys could prove ; and that taking into account the probabilities of a different level of the land, a wooded condition of the country, a greater rainfall, and a glacial filling in of the Somme Valley with clay and stones, subsequently cut out by running water, the gravels could scarcely be older than the Abbeville peat." Dr. Dawson in like manner fails to perceive,— and believes American geologists will agree with him,—any evidence of great antiquity in the caves of England or Belgium, the kitchen middens of Denmark, the rock shelters of France, or the lake habitations of Switzerland. He also speaks of Dr. Andrews' observations on the raised beaches of Lake Michigan, observations which have been much more precise than any made in Europe, enabling him to calculate that North America rose out of the waters of the glacial period between 5,500 and 7,500 years ago, and thus fixing the duration of the human period in America ; there are other lines of evidence which would reduce the residence of man to a much shorter period ; longer periods have been deduced from the deposits at the delta of the Mississippi, *but Hilgard has found them to be in great part marine.*— [Ed.]

[*] Sir John Lubbock has suggested the terms *Palæolithic* and *Neolithic* for the two main divisions of the Stone age. Implements of the Palæolithic

put forward as to there being a broad line of distinction to be drawn between implements found in the gravel and those that belong to the Neolithic, or surface period ; but I must say that I do not see such a marvellous difference as he sees in the character of the chipping of the two periods. It is true that the chipping of the earlier period is such as we might ordinarily expect from man in a low degree of civilization ; but, occasionally, in the older deposits, we find instruments as beautifully chipped at the edges as those of the later period ; while, on the other hand, in the Neolithic, or surface period, we occasionally find instruments as rudely, or even more rudely chipped, than many of those which belong to the gravel, or the Palæo- lithic period. It is but reasonable to suppose that where a flint was taken merely to serve some temporary purpose, the point, or edge, was just chipped into form, and that when it had served the object for which it was intended, it was thrown aside as no longer of any use, in the same way as, up to within the last twenty or thirty years, flints used to be taken and roughly chipped into form, in order to be placed in the tinder-box to serve for obtaining a light in the morning ; and I have no doubt that many of these roughly-chipped flints do belong to the "strike-a-light" period. I have here two implements chipped in the same manner, so that Mr. Michell would say there is no difference traceable in them. One is of the Palæolithic period, and is, I conclude, intended to be used at the point, and the other is a hatchet of the Neolithic period, dexterously ground to an edge at one end. I think it would be impossible to get two implements presenting more precisely the

---

period are formed by the process of chipping only ; no single instance of finishing them by artificial rubbing has been observed. During the Neolithic period some of the flint and stone implements, such as hatchets and axes, after having been chipped into shape, were finished by artificial rubbing or polishing, whilst many others, such as arrow-heads and scrapers, were still formed by the process of flaking and chipping only. The implements of the Palæolithic differ greatly in form from those of the Neolithic period. No implements of characteristic Neolithic types have been found under circum- stances enabling us to assign them to the Palæolithic period, but the reverse cannot be asserted, although cases are rare. (*Flint Chips*, by Stevens, p. 34.) Dr. Dawson, in his *Earth and Man*, says :—"In England all before the Roman invasion is prehistoric ; the evidence of this period is chiefly geo- logical in character ; the prehistoric men are essentially fossils ; we know of them merely from what can be learned from their bones and implements embedded in the earth, or caverns ; for the origin of these the antiquary goes to the geologist, and imitates him in arranging his human fossils under such names as the 'Palæolithic,' or period of rude stone implements [to some this particular definition has seemed scarce satisfactory.—Ed.] ; the 'Neolithic,' or period of polished stone implements ; the Bronze period, and the Iron period ; though inasmuch as the higher and lower state of the arts seem always to have coexisted, and the time involved is comparatively short, these periods are of less value than those of geology. In Britain, the Iron age is mainly historic, the Bronze goes back to the time of early Phœ- nician trade, and the Stone reaches further back. In Western Asia, the Bronze and Iron ages are 2,000 years earlier than in Britain, while in America, the Palæolithic age of chipped stone implements still continues."—[Ed.]

same characteristics, but at the same time belonging to two totally different periods. I have here a stone which in form is a purely Palæolithic implement, characterized by the rude chipping of the period, and in all its essential features it is similar to the implements found in the drift; but I happen to be able to give you the origin of it, for I chipped it myself with a round pebble. With regard to Mr. Michell's argument that has been brought forward as to sand having the power of chipping flint, there is no doubt that sand does possess a certain polishing power, and in many instances, in the case of implements found in sandy beds, they are observed to have a very fine polish on their surfaces; but that polish always follows the lines of the chipping by which the implement was originally fashioned; and in the case of the flints exhibited by Mr. Michell, you may see, in some instances, the impression of the bulbs of percussion, showing where the splinters have been dislodged in the shaping of the implements; while in others you may see the lines of the conchoidal fracture, preserved by the action of sand. I think I have now said enough to show what are the views held on this subject by myself, views which I think Mr. Whitley has in one or two cases misapprehended.

Mr. WHITLEY.—I have not the honour of being a member of this Institute, but I have brought from Cornwall a great number of the flints which you see on the table, and which I have collected during the past ten years. I have had the opportunity, in the prosecution of my profession as an engineer, of observing the mode in which they are distributed, and the extent to which they are deposited over the whole of the south-west of England. In addition to this, I have taken a good deal of interest in the subject we are discussing, and the result of my investigations has been to convince my own mind that a mistake has been made by some of our scientific men. With all due respect for the opinions of those who differ from me, and for the high and prominent names by which this flint implement theory has been supported, I have come to a conclusion contrary to that at which they have arrived, and think I have good reason on my side for believing that these so-called implements have been formed by natural causes, and not by the hand of man. (Hear.) I am more accustomed to the field-work of an engineer, than to addressing an audience in a room like this, and I trust you will excuse me if I do not refer in detail to all that Mr. Evans has said with regard to myself; but I do say most confidently, that I have been very careful not to misquote him, and on all occasions to refer to my authorities where it has been necessary. If he will adduce any instance of a misquotation, I shall at once, with the greatest pleasure and sincerity of purpose, acknowledge my error. Mr. Evans has done me the honour to refer to the arguments which, simply and plainly, I have used against the implement theory. I have observed in my paper, and, I believe, on Mr. Evans's authority and that of Sir John Lubbock, that all the implements of the Palæolithic period are made of flint, and I think if I were to search their works I should be able to certify that this is their opinion as well as mine.* The only evidence Mr. Evans has given that I have made a mistake on this point, is that there are implements found in Madras which are said to be quartzite.

Mr. EVANS.—I also mentioned one from Brandon that was made of felsite or greenstone.

Mr. WHITLEY.—I think it probable that it was of chert. There are a great many varieties of flint, and we should take care not to be misled on this subject by a particular variety of the mineral. Chert is a variety of flint, and when Mr. Evans refers to the quartzite of India, everybody knows that all the implements of the greensand are chert implements. There are upon the table some chert implements which I obtained from the greensand round Axminster, and there are some flakes by their side which have come from Pressigny-le-Grand, which will illustrate what I have stated. I have also to refer to another point, and that is with regard to the great number of these so-called implements. I have stated that these implements are so great in number as to lead to the conclusion that they must have been produced by natural causes, and not by the hand of man. At St. Acheul I searched the gravel-beds, and it is a fact that, from three acres of land at that place, no fewer than 3,000 of these "tools" have been exhumed, or an average of 1,000 axes per acre! I ask, whether any one could expect to find in any river-bed, in any part of the world, as many as ten lost axes, even in the neighbourhood of a large town? (Hear.) Now, 1,000 lost axes per acre would give a total of 640,000 in a square mile, and as these beds are scattered throughout the valley of the Somme for twenty miles, you will find, on making a calculation, that the proportion of lost axes to the number of savages would be about six million to one! (Hear, hear.) As I have come three hundred miles to attend this meeting, I should like to lay some of the main facts of the case before the audience I have the honour of addressing, trusting that in doing so you will kindly bear with my imperfections as a speaker. In carrying out the engineering works in which I have been engaged in North Devon, I walked to Croyde, an exposed cliff on the western shore, and there I found what are termed by some "bundles of flakes," and what others call "nests of flakes," on the soil above the seashore. I stated this fact in a paper which Professor Huxley did me the honour of reading before the Geological Society, and I have been told that I made a great mistake, and that what I had seen was the site of a manufactory! Several gentlemen have since been down and examined those flakes at Croyde, and they declare that there has been a manufactory there of Palæolithic

---

* Mr. Evans says, "The material from which all the implements hitherto discovered in the drift of this country and of the north of France have been formed, is the flint derived from the chalk." (*Archæologia*, vol. xxxix. p. 64 (1865 ?).) Again—"that in the Palæolithic period—the material used in Europe was, moreover, as far as at present known, almost exclusively flint." (*Ancient Stone Implements*, p. 49 (1872).) Sir John Lubbock says, of the drift implements, "All those hitherto discovered are made of flint." (*Prehistoric Times*, 1st ed., p. 270 (1865).)

tools ! As my duties kept me in that locality for some years, I explored the whole country round. I was engaged in embanking, making roads, and in draining land, and I found that these flakes were scattered through the sub-soil over an area of about twenty miles in length and ten miles in breadth, and yet I am told that this was " a manufactory of Palæolithic tools " ! Now, I will ask you to consider this theory in relation to one fact to which I will call attention. The manufactory required for the whole of the British navy at Keyham covers an area of just one square mile. According to those who say that these flakes at Croyde and its neighbourhood are evidence of a manufactory for a few scattered savages, the manufactory must have covered an area of two hundred square miles ! I put it to the common sense of those whom I am addressing,—could this have been a manufactory ? What to my mind is certain, and what I am ready to prove against all comers, is this : that these flint flakes have a geological and not an antiquarian origin. (Hear, hear.) Walking along the seashore, it can be seen that the flakes, which are found in the subsoil inland, and there supposed to be " nests of flakes," are ex-posed in cliff sections, and may thus be traced for a considerable distance along the shore-line. I traced these flakes from the Scilly Isles, and found the drift of shattered flints again at the Land's End, where they are scattered over an area of seven miles in length. I traced them beyond this to different places, namely, St. Ives, St. Agnes, Padstow, Hartland Point, and several of the headlands in that district and beyond Ilfracombe. I traced them, also, across the Channel to Caldy Island, and along the south coast of Wales ; and Sir Roderick Murchison has indicated by his map that these flakes are found on the western coast of Wales. They are scattered on the Isle of Man, and you may follow them until you come to the very spot where they originate, in the county of Antrim, at Carrickfergus, and Larne. In fact, on the other side of the Irish Sea, these so-called flint "implements" are scattered along the eastern coast of Ireland from Antrim as far as Ballycotton Bay in the county of Cork. This certainly looks as if we had found the origin of the flakes ; but there is more con-clusive evidence yet. The flint drift of Antrim is known by three well-recognized marks. In connection with this drift we find the indurated chalk known as the white limestone—a peculiar kind of limestone found in the north of Ireland, hardened by basalt. I have found at Scilly frequent examples of the basalt, and I have also noticed among those islands some of the burnt flints, such as are found at Antrim between the basalt and the chalk ; so that in this threefold cord, which cannot be easily broken, you may trace the origin of these flints to Antrim as surely and as completely as you can trace the origin of the negro to Africa. (Hear, hear.) And it should be noticed that these flints are not carried and scattered about as they would be if they had been used as gun-flints, or, in earlier times, as arrow-heads, but they are found in a regular geological stratum about two feet below the soil ; and what is more remarkable still, throughout the whole of Cornwall, as every surveying engineer in that part of the country knows, you will find under the soil a stratum of shattered quartz and hard stones which have somehow been broken and smashed up. With these broken quartz the flint-flakes are found mixed. Leaving Cornwall, and coming to Cissbury-hill, the flint-flakes are found in a thick stratum, and in cart-loads, about two feet under the soil on each side of the hill. I went to Belgium, and at Spiennes, near Mons, I found these flakes most abundant. I found them in the village at the top of the gardens, and two or three feet below the surface of the soil there was a stratum of most perfect flakes, with the bulb of percussion plainly developed, and all the usual marks of "chipping." This stratum was six inches thick, and I traced it for more than a quarter of a mile along the country. And not only was this the case, but I found that by denudation these flakes were scattered over the soil in the lower district. Certainly, when you look at one of these flakes, and at the way in which it is chipped—and consider that the antiquaries say that all the blows were delivered on one end, and for one purpose—there does appear to be some reason to think that they have not been formed by natural causes; but it happens that I am engaged in making roads and in doing engineering works at Eastbourne, and my contractor there prepares the metalling for the roads by crushing large nodules of flint with one of Blake's stone-breakers. There are two men engaged in shovelling in the flints, and as fast as they can feed the crushing machine, the great iron jaw, which is worked by a steam-engine, crushes the pieces. From these crushed flints which are manipulated by this powerful and unintellectual crusher, I can pick out flint-flakes and "cores" in any number. On those flakes, you will see the bulb of percussion, the marks of chipping, and every evidence of manufacture as perfectly demonstrated as they are on the flakes which Mr. Evans sets down as having been formed by human agency. I say this advisedly and with great respect for all who differ from me. I will only make a few further remarks. Mr. Evans has rather taken the wind out of my sails by the course he has taken in answering my arguments; but I am quite certain of this, that none of these implements, nor of those which have been brought from St. Acheul, nor any that are on the table in this room, bear the same marks of use upon them as the Neolithic implements bear. Mr. Evans has put it very strongly that they do bear marks of use; but he did not say that the marks of use on the Palæolithic tools were of the same character as the marks of use which are observable on the Neolithic implements. I have seen and examined in the museums at Abbeville and Salisbury, and in the gravel-beds of Norfolk and elsewhere, probably more than a thousand of these flint implements, and I am able to declare with great honesty and sincerity that I have not been able to find a single implement that bears the same kind of marks of use which are borne by the Neolithic tools.* If you will allow me, I will endeavour to illustrate

---

* The following seems to give indirect support to the views Mr. Whitley holds :— "To Dr. Hooker I have been indebted for some examples of stones, the first specimens of which were picked up by Mr. Hackworth on the shores of Lyell's Bay, New Zealand. . . . The stones, which have a strong resem-

this point. Here is a Neolithic implement (producing it) found near Abbeville, and the indications of use upon it are obvious. There are the marks of grinding on the surface, and the instrument looks as if its point had been worn back, while there is an indentation as if it had been rubbed by a thong. This, I admit, is as obviously a work of art as any "Sheffield whittle"; but I have not found, and I must add that I do not think Mr. Evans can find, the same marks of use on the Palæolithic tools. I know that Mr. Evans says they do bear marks giving evidence of wear; but I say that what he calls wear may have arisen from friction and attrition in a gravel-bed as well as from their having been used by man; and, furthermore, Mr. Evans does not say that they always show marks of having been so used, which, of course, is quite a different thing from attrition in a gravel-bed. However, in some cases Mr. Evans does attempt to prove that there are marks of wear on these flints as exhibited by the serrated edges. In reply to this, I wish to call attention to the fact that all the marks of wear found on the Neolithic tools are shown in the smoothness of edge which has resulted from use; but in the case of the Palæolithic tools the evidence of use relied on by Mr. Evans has been the jagged edges. (Hear, hear.) I would here refer to the circumstance that in the criticism Mr. Evans has made on my pamphlet, he does not controvert that portion of it in which I assert that " no relics of man are found in the drift with the so-called implements." I repeat again, that no such relics are found in the gravel-beds mixed up with the Palæolithic tools. You are all aware of the intense interest that was excited by the human jawbone which was said to have been discovered by Boucher de Perthes at some depth in the gravel at Abbeville; but after the examination which was made of that jaw by Dr. Falconer and other scientific gentlemen well able to pronounce an authoritative opinion on such a subject, that jaw has been put on one side, and can no longer be admitted into the controversy.* (Hear.) There is another point to which I might refer in connection with this subject, and that is, that wherever the other works of man are found along with his implements, they are found only upon the surface and not in the drift. For instance, in the valleys of Switzerland, we find that the ancient people who lived in those lake districts have left behind

———————

blance to works of human art, occur in great abundance, and of various sizes, from half an inch to several inches in length. A large number were exhibited, showing the various forms, which are those of wedges, knives, arrow-heads, &c., and all with sharp cutting edges. . . . Dr. Hector stated, that although, as a group, the specimens on the table could not well be mistaken for artificial productions; still the forms are so peculiar, and the edges, in a few of them, so perfect, that if they were discovered associated with human works, there is no doubt that they would have been referred to the so-called 'Stone period.' "—Professor Tyndall in *Macmillan's Magazine* for May, 1873, p. 57.

* One of the teeth being extracted and examined, was found to be not yet dry!—[Ed.]

33

them not only their flint tools,[*] but remnants even of their food—the baked corn they used to eat—as well as the raiment they used to wear, their ornaments, pieces of their pottery, and a number of other things, which abundantly prove man's existence there ; but when we go to the gravel-beds we find no other relic of man than these so-called Palæolithic flint tools, if I am to except the necklaces of the Palæolithic girls—(laughter)—which have been found in the gravel-beds of St. Acheul. I have upon the table a few of these beads, which are said to have been the work of man. Here (producing several specimens) are some of them. These sub-globular sponges have been examined by Professor Rupert Jones and Dr. Carpenter, and pronounced by them to be fossil organisms of the chalk, which Professor Jones says can be found in abundance in the chalk, " either in the perforated condition, or solid, or with a more or less shallow hole in their substance." This being so, I say that it is a cruel thing to arrange these fossils on a string in the form of a necklace and dangle them (here Mr. Whitley held up a string of the fossils) before the eyes of the uninformed as relics of Palæolithic man. (Laughter and applause.) I must not trespass much further on your time ; but may state that there are many implements here in reference to which I am quite ready to offer any explanations that may be needed, and shall at all times be willing to meet and answer any one on this subject. I trust that I shall always be able with honesty and good temper, and at least with some scientific skill, to argue the question, and I repeat that my strong impression is, from an intelligent inspection, that both these beads and these Palæolithic implements have been produced by natural causes, and not by the hand of man. There is just one other point to which I should like to refer before sitting down. There are upon the table a great number of discs, which are termed " discoidal implements " by Mr. Stevens, and he tells us that they are sometimes found chipped into form so as to make very good Palæolithic missiles. Now, these things are very common. Here is a great piece of chert that I picked up, and on every side of it you may see little cups, which it is contended are evidence of the chipping where the " discoidal implement" has been broken into shape. Here is another specimen, also of a large size. Now, if you look at these pieces of flint, you will see little cups broken all over them, and these little cups have all been acknowledged by those who have examined them to be perfectly natural. Here is a beautiful one from Pressigny-le-Grand, and numbers of them are found scattered all over Norfolk. One of them is so small that it might be used as a button of the smallest size ; and here is another from Eastbourne, so large that it could hardly be put into the pocket. It only requires a careful inspection to prove that these marks on the flint are all produced by natural causes. Here is a most beautiful flint knife from the Taw, which has all the marks of

---

[*] Professor E. H. Palmer, in his admirable work, *The Desert of the Exodus*, found the same implements at the mines which were worked by the Egyptians at the time of the Exodus.—[Ed.]

(1-8)

chipping, but no one can say that it has been formed by man. My last search was made at Axminster on Saturday. On one side of the table there are twenty tools, which I then discovered, and which would be called Palæolithic if they had been found in Brixham cavern ; in the course of one hour I picked them all up in one field, and the " cores " are in every way as good and as perfect as those which Mr. Evans has drawn in his work, and which were found in one of the Indian rivers. (Applause.)

Dr. W. B. CARPENTER, F.R.S.—In appearing here to say a few words on this subject, I wish it to be understood that I am not about to address myself to the general question. I am not a geologist, neither can I call myself an archæologist ; but I do wish to say a few words upon the general question of evidence, because that is a subject to which I have paid special attention. In my address, as President of the British Association at Brighton, I said that this was one of those questions in which common sense was superior to logic. Mr. Whitley has given us a good deal of common sense to-night ; and as far as he has done that, I go along with him. I have taken some pains to study what is called common sense, and to endeavour to arrive at what it really is, and how we are to get at it ; and if any one wants to know what are my opinions on this subject, he will find them in an article which I wrote, a year and a half ago, in the *Contemporary Review*. I there stated that logicians had come to no agreement as to the sources of our knowledge of the external world ; that every logical proof which the greatest logicians, such as Sir William Hamilton and others, have attempted to give of the existence of an external world,— or of such a proposition as that I am here among a number of persons, and that to say so is not a mere fallacy evolved out of my own consciousness,—has been invalidated by some other logician ; and yet, I ask, who can disbelieve the fact ? Our belief in such a case is based entirely on common sense ; and what I call common sense I will briefly define as the general resultant of the whole previous training and discipline of our minds. In certain things, as to which we all agree, common sense is sufficient for all of us, because our minds are all so constituted that we come to the same conclusions with regard to them ; as, for instance, upon the question of the existence of an external world. There are, however, other cases in which the trained common sense of men who have made special departments of science their study, lead those who have so trained themselves to very positive conclusions, which may and often do appear unsound or even absurd to such as have not studied these special subjects. For example, the remarkable results of the spectroscope, to those who have not mastered the scientific principles by which they have been arrived at, may seem preposterous. It may appear absurd to say that a jet of incandescent hydrogen, fifty miles high, shall burst out from the sun and disappear in ten minutes, this assertion being made on the strength of two or three fine red lines shown in the spectroscope ; and yet no person who has made a special study of the subject has the least doubt about it. To me it seems that no person who has used his common sense, without any previous prejudice, can come to any other conclusion, when he sees a whole series of objects like those Mr. Evans has produced, than that they have been the work of human design, and intended for special purposes. (Hear.) It is true that each individual blow upon one of these flints, taken by itself, might be regarded as an accidental fracture; but when we take up one of the implements and see the definite and symmetrical contour that has been given to it, the manner in which the different blows have been made in succession so as to produce a regular and uniform edge, and when, in addition to this, we see that several of these tools are declared to have all been taken out of the same gravel-bed, and when we observe the same general conditions attaching to all of them, and especially when we find them made out of different materials, it certainly does appear to me that common sense can only point to the one conclusion,—that they have had a human origin. (Hear.) And here I will give you an example as to the value of common-sense judgment, which I think every one will be able to appreciate. I remember hearing, a few years ago, a statement of the circumstances under which a man was enabled to trace a lost purse. He was robbed of his money, and the man who committed the theft ran away. The supposed thief was caught, and a purse was found upon him, which, however, he declared was his own. The man who had lost the purse could not swear to it, as it was of a common type, but he was able to say exactly how much money was in the purse of which he had been robbed, and he named the precise sum. He was further asked, "Do you know what form the money was in?" and he replied, "Yes; there were a half-sovereign, a half-crown, a florin, three shillings and two sixpences." He happened to remember, having taken some change not long before, that that was the precise amount of the money, and the precise form in which he had received it. The jury found unhesitatingly and upon the moment that the purse and the money were his, and I think that any one I am now addressing would have done the same. Now, I apply the argument I have been using to this case; for although any individual sixpence, or shilling, or half-crown might have been in another purse than that of which the man had been robbed, yet the concurrence in this case of the precise number and amount of the different pieces in the purse, and their identity in these respects with what the prosecutor had lost, were so convincing that the conviction could not be resisted. It appears to me that this is precisely the kind of judgment on which we should come to a decision on such a subject as we are now discussing. I cannot myself conceive any other conclusion that is to be drawn from the premises. I do not lay the least stress on the general question to which Mr. Whitley has directed attention to-night, as to whether certain flint-flakes are natural or artificial; for it never appeared to me that they had anything like the same amount of evidence in favour of their human origin, as is furnished by the more perfect implements.*

---

* With regard to what has been said as to the flint flakes, I would remark that before we can form any definite conclusion, we must set the numbers of the supposed flint implements against the supposed indications that they have

A flake may be made by accidental blows. This flake, for instance (taking up one) has only three fractured surfaces upon it : on this (taking up another) there are two or three. But here is an " implement" on which I should not, perhaps, be wrong in saying there are 150 fractures, and I ask, is it conceivable that 150 fractures could be made to produce such an object as this by any natural or accidental process ?* (Hear, hear.) It may be conceivable to some minds, but it is inconceivable to mine. Having been trained to the study of evidence, I find it, I repeat, inconceivable that this object could have been made except by design, and for a special purpose. The matter is one of common sense, and the common sense of mankind agrees in one conclusion. I do not base my argument on any opposition to Mr. Whitley's conclusion, that all these small flakes have been made by natural causes ; but I base it on these highly-elaborated artificial implements from the Somme valley gravel-beds.† There is another point on which I might make a few observations. I find that not only in the paper of this evening, but likewise in other works which have appeared on the same side, it is imputed over and over again that scientific men have gone into this subject with a prejudice ; and they are charged with a scientific cliquism which prevents their accepting the truth in this matter ! Now, if I were to go

---

been formed by man. If they are to be found in such enormous numbers, if they can be arranged in a series varying from the most imperfect to the most perfect forms, if they can be produced by flint-crushers, it would be necessary that we should possess the most certain evidence that no power of nature was adequate for their formation before we could arrive at the conclusion on principles of common sense that the fact of their human origin was proved. —[Rev. Preb. C. A. Row, M.A.]

* The first flint Dr. Carpenter took up was one which Mr. Whitley and Mr. Michell held to belong to the Palæolithic age, and to be naturally chipped ; as to the second, no one in the room thought of disputing the fact that it was manufactured. The whole contention, on the part of Mr. Michell, Mr. Whitley, and others, was in regard to the first.—[ED.]

† The genuineness of some of these implements has been more than questioned. Mr. Keeping, a practical geologist, who went over to Abbeville, says he spent a week with a pickaxe searching in vain for implements ; and the Honorary Secretary of the Geological and Numismatic Societies wrote as follows to Mr. Prestwich as to the honesty of some of the workmen :—" The proofs I gave in my former letter were, I think, sufficient to show that a regular system of imposition has been carried on by the gravel-diggers of Abbeville ; that the majority of implements lately obtained at Moulin Quignon are false. . . . But if more conclusive evidence of fraud be required, I am now prepared to give it." And Mr. Evans, writing in the Athenæum, 6th June, 1863, said :—" Genuine implements have been hitherto comparatively rare at Moulin Quignon. The suspected implements are now found in abundance." The rarity of those implements which Mr. Evans holds to be genuine may be gathered from the following extract from Flint Chips, by E. T. Stevens (p. 39) :—" In April, 1857, Mr. Prestwich and Mr. J. Evans inspected the Abbeville beds, under the guidance of M. Boucher de Perthes ; and at Amiens, Mr. Prestwich and Mr. Evans saw one of the pear-shaped flint implements in situ. In the same year Mr. J. W. Flowers found a pear-shaped implement in situ at Amiens. Shortly afterwards Mr. James Wyatt and Mr. T. Rupert Jones were equally fortunate."—[ED.]

into the real history of this inquiry, I think I could show that there has, upon the contrary, been great resistance on the part of the scientific men to the acceptance of the views they now entertain, and that these views have only been forced upon them by the weight of evidence. (Hear.) A Roman Catholic priest, Mr. J. MacEnery, worked out the subject thirty years ago. He found flint implements in Kent's Hole associated with the bones of extinct animals, and he wrote an account of the discovery and had plates drawn, which he sent up to Dr. Buckland. What did Dr. Buckland say? How did he treat the matter? Did he at once bring it out as a grand new scientific discovery,—as one that he welcomed and was glad to put before the world? On the contrary, he persuaded Mr. MacEnery to keep the matter quiet; and the result was that his paper did not appear until after Mr. Prestwich's researches in the valley of the Somme had brought the matter before the scientific world in a manner that was not to be resisted. Did the researches of M. Boucher de Perthes meet with approval in the first instance?* Why, nobody thought anything of them until Dr. Falconer, while passing through the neighbourhood in which M. de Perthes' museum was, thought he might as well take a look in, and there he found that which satisfied him that there really was something worthy of investigation. Did Sir Charles Lyell show any disposition to accept heretical conclusions, when he visited the caverns of Liège, five-and-twenty years ago, and found human bones in the same deposit and condition of penetration by minerals, as the bones of extinct animals? When the professors there pointed out to him that there was just the same evidence of antiquity in the human bones as in the others, did he accept their reasoning? No; but he blamed himself ten or fifteen years afterwards for his incredulity. He said, "I ought to have accepted that evidence," and he regretted his former want of belief when the later testimony was flashed upon him. Did one of the scientific Englishmen, who went over to Abbeville to discuss that question of the human jaw, show himself desirous to bring forward heretical opinions, when they all took the side of those who were endeavouring to prove, and who did prove, ultimately, that that jaw was a

---

* M. Boucher de Perthes does not seem to have been without his own doubts upon the subject, for we read in his *Antiquités Celtiques*, tom. iii. p. 11 :--" J'y voyais des haches, et je voyais juste, mais la coupe en était vague et les angles émoussés ; leur forme aplatie différait de celle des haches polies, les seules que l'on connût alors ; enfin, si des traces de travail s'y révélaient, il fallait réellement, pour les voir, avoir les yeux de la foi. Je les avais, mais je les avais seul : ma doctrine s'étendait peu, je n'avais pas un seul disciple." "I traced the hand of man in the hatchets, and I judged rightly, but the proof of the workmanship was dubious, and the angles were blunted ; the broad shape of the tools differed from that of the polished hatchets which alone were then known. In short, if the traces of human work were to be seen, it was indispensable to the perception of them to have the eyes of faith. I had them, but I alone had them. My opinion found little favour ; I had not a single disciple."—[Ed.]

"plant"? (Laughter.) I can assure this meeting that there never was a question more thoroughly and completely sifted by arguments, coolly and dispassionately, but earnestly advanced. For two whole days this question of the jaw was discussed, and the whole subject of these flint implements was brought up ; but not a single scientific man belonging either to England or to France contested the human origin of those implements, or had the smallest doubt of it. A set of flint implements were produced, which there were strong reasons to believe had been made by modern workmen, and planted in the bed to give authenticity to the jaw. Those flint implements were carefully washed and examined, and compared with the undoubtedly genuine implements, which had been taken out of undisturbed gravel-beds, and which showed the most unmistakable evidence of age.* The fictitious

---

* Dr. Dawson, F.R.S., remarks, in his work, *Archaia :*—"It may be anticipated that almost every year will produce supposed cases of human remains or works of art in the later tertiary deposits. There are so many causes of accidental intermixtures, and ordinary observers are so little aware of the sources of error against which it is necessary to guard, that mistakes of this kind are inevitable. Even geologists are very likely to be misled in investigations of this nature. A remarkable instance of this, in the case of the delta of the Nile, has been already noticed. Another discovery, which has lately made some noise in the scientific world, is probably referable to the same category. I refer to the supposed occurrences of implements of flint in the gravel at Abbeville, in France. This was first maintained by M. Boucher de Perthes in 1849; but his statements appeared so improbable that little attention was given to them. More recently, Mr. Prestwich and Mr. Evans have brought the subject before the Royal Society and the Society of Antiquaries in England, in connection with the discovery of flint weapons with bones of extinct animals in a cave at Brixham.

"1. The implements found are described as follows by Mr. Evans, as reported in the *Athenæum :*—

"' 1. Flakes of flint, apparently intended for knives or arrow-heads. 2. Pointed implements, usually truncated at the base, and varying in length from four to nine inches—possibly used as spear or lance-heads, which in shape they resemble. 3. Oval or almond-shaped implements, from two to nine inches in length, and with a cutting edge all round. They have generally one end more sharply curved than the other, and occasionally even pointed, and were possibly used as sling-stones, or as axes, cutting at either end, with a handle bound round the centre. The evidence derived from the implements of the first form is not of much weight, on account of the extreme simplicity of the implements, which at times renders it difficult to determine whether they are produced by art or by natural causes. This simplicity of form would also prevent the flint-flakes made at the earliest period from being distinguishable from those of a later date. The case is different with the other two forms of implements, of which numerous specimens were exhibited ; all indisputably worked by the hand of man, and not indebted for their shape to any natural configuration or peculiar fracture of the flint. They present no analogy in form to the well-known implements of the so-called Celtic or Stone period, which, moreover, have for the most part some portion, if not the whole, of their surface ground or polished, and are frequently made from other stones than flint. Those from the Drift are, on the contrary, never ground, and are exclusively of flint. They have, indeed, every appearance of having been fabricated by another race of men, who,

implements, which had been manufactured by workmen, and had had a good colour given to their surface by being buried in the dark ferruginous sand, were found to be quite clean, new, and sharp ; but the genuine implements were penetrated with iron infiltration, and their edges showed distinct marks of having been used. No one has mentioned to-night what struck me as one of the most curious specimens in M. Boucher de Perthes' museum. One of the flint implements presented the rough Palæolithic form on one side, having been blocked out by blows ; while not only was the other side polished, but there was by the side of it the very stone on which it had been polished, as could be proved by the perfect fitting of the one to the other. Those two stones were found very near together in the gravel-beds of the Somme valley. There is only one point further that I should like to advert to. As I have said before, scientific men have been charged with a desire to go against the received beliefs on these subjects.

from the fact that the Celtic stone weapons have been found in the superficial soil above the Drift containing these rude weapons, as well as from other considerations, must have inhabited this region of the globe at a period anterior to its so-called Celtic occupation.'

"The objects found are here admitted to differ from the implements of the primitive Celts, and they differ in like manner from those of the American Indians, which are almost if not quite undistinguishable from those of ancient Europe and Asia. One at least of the kinds mentioned has scarcely a semblance of artificial form, and the others are all merely fractured, not ground or polished. In so far as one can judge, without actually inspecting the specimens, these appear to be fatal defects in their claim to be weapons. The observers have evidently not taken into consideration the effects of intense frost in splitting flinty and jaspery stones. It is easy to find, among the *débris* of the jasper veins of Nova Scotia, for instance, abundance of ready-made arrow-heads and other weapons ; and there is every reason to believe that the Indians, and perhaps the aboriginal Celts also, sought for and found those naturally split stones which gave them the least trouble in the manufacture, just as they selected beach pebbles of suitable forms for anchors, pestles and hammers, and hard slates with oblique joints for knives. To these natural forms, however, the savage usually adds a little polishing, notching, or other adaptation ; and this seems to be wanting in the greater part of the specimens from Abbeville.

" 2. Nothing is more difficult, especially in an uneven country, than to ascertain the extent to which old gravels have been re-arranged by earthquake waves or land floods. Nor does the occurrence in them of bones of extinct animals prove anything, since these are shifted with the gravel. Very careful and detailed observations of the locality would be required to attain any certainty on this point.

" 3. The places in which gravel-pits are dug, are often just those to which the aborigines are likely to have resorted for their supply of flint weapons. They may have burrowed in the gravel for that purpose, and their pits may have been subsequently filled up. Further, savages generally make their implements as near as possible to the places where they procure the raw material ; and in making flint weapons, where the material abounds, they reject without scruple all except those that are most easily worked into form. If of human origin at all, the so-called weapons of Abbeville are more like such rejectamenta than perfected implements. This would also account for the

I reply that, so far from this being the case, they have resisted the evidence put before them as long as they could ; but let me inform this meeting as to what a most eminent scientific man, and a most firm believer in those views as to the authority of the Scriptures, which this Society desires to maintain —I allude to the late Dr. Prichard—thought ; and what was his judgment on the general question of the Antiquity of Man before this particular part of the subject came up. It is remarkable that physiologists have long been coming to the conclusion, that if you are to limit to a few hundred years the period of man's existence on this earth before the Exodus, commencing from the period usually assigned to the Deluge, it is difficult to imagine how the three distinct forms of the human race, exhibited by the Negro, the Egyptian, and the Jew, all of which are so clearly and definitely shown in the paintings of ancient Egypt, could have arisen in so short a space of time. (Hear.)* Dr. Prichard was a very firm advocate of the doctrine of the unity of the human race, and the derivation of the whole of that race from one common stock. He wrote a most learned and laborious work on the subject, and the last

---

quantity found, which would otherwise seem to be inconsistent with the supposition of human workmanship.

"4. The circumstance that no bones or other remains referable to man have been found with the flint articles, is more in accordance with the suppositions stated above, than with that of their human origin, in any other way than as the rejectamenta of an ancient manufacture.

"5. From a summary of the facts given by Sir Charles Lyell at a meeting of the British Association (1859), as the result of personal investigations, it appears that the gravels in question are *fluviatile* and dependent on the present valley of the Somme, though still apparently of very great antiquity. This places the subject in an entirely different position from that in which it was left by Perthes and Prestwich. River gravels are often composed of older *débris*, re-assorted in a comparatively short time, and containing tertiary remains intermixed with those that are modern ; and it is usually quite impossible to determine their age with certainty. Further, if we may judge from American rivers, those of France must, when the country was covered with forest, have been much larger than at present ; and at the same time their annual freshets must have been smaller, so that nothing is more natural than that remains of the savage aborigines should be found in beds now far removed from the action of the rivers. When to this we add the occurrence at intervals of great river inundations, we cannot, without a series of investigations bearing on the effects of all these changes, allow any great antiquity to be claimed for such deposits. The subject is, in short, in such a condition at present, that nothing can with safety be affirmed with respect to it.

"I may add that Sir Charles Lyell, while admitting the apparent contemporaneous association of human remains with those of extinct animals of the Tertiary period at Brixham, rejects as modern the so-called fossil men of Denise in central France, which had been associated with the Abbeville discoveries."

* Dr. Kitchen Parker, F.R.S., President of the Microscopical Society, whilst dissatisfied with the modern view of the Chronology of Genesis, yet has called my attention to the distinct race that the Americans are becoming, how a short time has produced a considerable change. He says, " The Yankee is a good subspecies already, and a very fine new type he is."—[ED.]

edition of his book came out in successive volumes. During the publication of this edition, it was reviewed by a very able critic, who brought as an objection to the doctrine, the impossibility of supposing that the divarication of races could have taken place in so short a time as is allowed by the usual chronology. In a long and learned note, Dr. Prichard goes into the question of what is the value of that chronology. Now, Dr. Prichard ranked as a physiologist among physiologists, as a philologist among philologists, and as a scholar among scholars ; and if any one will read the long note at the end of the fifth volume of his great work on the *Physical History of Man*, he will be impressed with Dr. Prichard's thorough honesty and sincerity, and his strong desire to arrive at the truth. Dr. Prichard came to this conclusion—that while we may assign tolerably definite dates to the Exodus and the call of Abraham, yet if we interpret the antecedent records according to the usages of Eastern genealogies, there is no basis whatever for the received chronology ; and he finishes with this remarkable expression —more remarkable from its having been used thirty years ago :—" Beyond that event, we can never know how many centuries, may have elapsed since the first man clay received the image of God and the breath of life." That was the judgment of a most honest, religious, and conscientious man, given on the basis of scientific and scholarly investigation, thirty years ago, before the present question came up.* (Hear, hear.) I do not say that I was not prepared, through having been Dr. Prichard's intimate friend, associated with him in scientific inquiry, and asked by him to write a review of his work in the *Edinburgh Review*, for the results of later researches ; I was quite ready to accept them ; but, on the other hand, I had no wish to accept and adopt them. I protest against the assumption that scientific men have entered upon the consideration of these subjects with any other than

---

* Dr. Carpenter seems to be under the delusion that it is a kind of new discovery to theologians that the popular chronology will not hold water. I can assure him that this is a complete mistake, and theologians have long been aware of its difficulties, and of the uncertainty of the evidence on which it rests. Probably there is no writer of reputation who would affirm that the so-called received chronology from the building of Solomon's Temple upwards can be made out on a basis which will carry conviction. It is notorious that we have three different systems of chronology in the Hebrew, Samaritan, and Greek copies of the Bible respectively, involving a large period of time ; and that the genealogical lists on which the popular chronology is founded are not complete. As to the real interval of time between the building of Solomon's Temple and the creation of man, theologians hold the utmost variety of opinion. As scientific men would object to be credited with popular opinions about science, and to be made responsible for them, so theologians ask at their hands that they will not credit them with the popular opinions about chronology. As also it is far from being the case that every person who volunteers to write on scientific subjects is a scientific man, so let not scientific men assume that every one who attempts to handle theological subjects is a theologian.—[Rev. Preb. C. A. Row, M.A.]

the one simple object of obtaining some addition to our knowledge of ancient man. There is an idea that men of science investigate scientific questions with a view of raising an antagonism to religion, and of forming a scientific clique to upset the Bible. This, to my mind, is a most unfair and unjust assertion, and one which I shall, on all proper occasions, feel it necessary to repudiate on the part of my scientific brethren and myself.* (Hear.) We simply go into this matter of the flints as a question of scientific truth and evidence, and are all just as ready to welcome facts on the one side as on the other. With regard to what Mr. Whitley has stated, I have learnt a great deal from him to-night. The subject of the diffusion of these flint-flakes, on which he has enlarged, has opened up a number of new questions with respect to the causes of that distribution. (Applause.)

----

* Dr. Carpenter for the moment appears to have forgotten that there is some foundation for the "idea"; no one will accuse him or men of science generally of antagonism to religion, but Dr. Carpenter, as President of the British Association, at Brighton, in 1872, found it necessary to speak as follows:—"When science, passing beyond its own limits, assumes to take the place of theology, and sets up its own conception of the order of nature as a sufficient account of its cause, it is invading a province of thought to which it has no claim, and not unreasonably provokes the hostility of those who ought to be its best friends."

Commenting upon these words in the Preface of Volume VI. of the *Transactions*, we said,—"Attacks on revealed religion tend to injure the progress of true science, and it would be well if those, whose scientific labours are otherwise of no small value, were deterred by Dr. Carpenter's remarks from continuing assaults made with the foregone conclusion that the Christian religion is unworthy of credence. Upon this subject generally, the Right Honourable W. E. Gladstone, in his address delivered at Liverpool College, in December, 1872, spoke as follows:— 'Belief cannot now be defended by reticence, any more than by railing, or by any privileges or assumptions. Nor, again, can it be defended exclusively by its 'standing army'—by priests and ministers of religion. To them, I do not doubt, will fall the chief share of the burden, and of the honour, and of the victory. But we commit a fatal error if we allow this to become a mere professional question. It is the affair of all. . . . . . The combat is now with men who commonly confess not only that Christianity has done good, but even that it may still confer at least some relative benefit before the day of perfect preparedness for its removal shall arrive ; and one of the most 'advanced' of whom . . . . appears to be touched by a lingering sentiment of tenderness, while he blows his trumpet for a final assault at once upon the 'Syrian superstition' and on the poor, pale, and semi-animate substitutes for it which Deism has devised. . . . . It is not now only the Christian Church, or only the Holy Scriptures, or only Christianity which is attacked. The disposition is boldly proclaimed to deal alike with root and branch, and to snap utterly the ties which, under the still venerable name of religion, unite man with the unseen world, and lighten the struggles and the woes of life by the hope of a better land. These things are done as the professed results, and the newest triumphs of modern thought and modern science ; but I believe that neither science nor thought is responsible, any more than liberty is responsible, for misdeeds committed in their names.'"—[ED.]

Capt. F. PETRIE.—Mr. Borlase will be called upon to speak on the other side ; but before the Chairman asks him to do so, I am anxious to say that we are in danger of going astray in the discussion, through a misconception with regard to the flint-flakes brought here by Mr. Evans, and which Dr. Carpenter asserts, in the name of common sense, to be artificial. Mr. Michell fully grants that they are, so will every one present ; but he holds that there is a great difference between them and the naturally-chipped flints of the Drift, in other words, he holds that there is a great difference between the flakes which are arranged on each side of the chairman ; the one set he holds as being naturally, the other artificially, chipped.

Mr. WILLIAM C. BORLASE.—I will confine my remarks to the smaller flint-flakes which are scattered broadcast over the surface of Cornwall. These, as a geologist, I have always considered as nothing more nor less than the insoluble residue of the soluble chalk. They are "*leavings*," not "*bringings*." In this opinion I have been confirmed by some recent remarks of Mr. Etheridge, who speaks of the cretaceous beds extending, in his belief, at one time over the whole of the west of England. "In Devonshire," he says, "we find piles of flint upon the upper greensand, the chalk being gone." In Cornwall, we find these flints broken—broken I cannot say how, but with the bulb of percussion sometimes shown upon them—along with pebbles of this very same upper greensand. There is one remarkable thing about them, and that is, that if any of you were to go to different parts of Cornwall, and put the flints you gathered there into three or four different piles, I could tell you the district from which each of them came, owing to the manner in which the colouring of the different beds has apparently affected them. I have found these flints in their simplest forms as flakes, not only on the surface, but in the barrows and urns of the dead, mixed up with the ashes of the funeral pyre, and in these cases sometimes they are artificially chipped ; but as a rule they are simple flakes, such as I see before me. Some of the flakes have been burnt with the ashes, and in these cases they may have been what Mr. Evans declares some of them to be—the "strike-a-lights" for the funeral pyre. But all we can gather from this is that man knew the whereabouts of these several deposits, and recognized their utility for the several purposes in which he could employ them, sometimes as a simple arrow-head, and sometimes as the means of striking a light for his fire. When he found that they were not quite suitable in shape, he may have chipped them a little, and thus it may be that we often find chipped ones along with the others. We find arrow-heads as good as those of Scotland, side by side with these simple little flakes ; but surely nature may sometimes be allowed to have rivalled the ingenuity of man, and to have imitated his handiwork so far as to form a simple flake. What others nature has left, man has wrought out more completely for his use.

Professor TENNANT.—I have very little to say upon this subject, except with reference to a statement that has been made as to the variety of materials of which implements are composed. This is due in reality to the localities in which they are found. If we go to New Zealand, we find that there they used jade; that in the Channel Islands they used basalt; in Mexico, the natives used obsidian, while in other countries substances of a like kind, chiefly siliceous, were employed in the formation of implements. With respect to the specimen in my hand, this was certainly not made by accidental causes. It is partly manufactured, and by no ordinary process of bringing two or more things accidentally together, could it have been converted into such a hatchet as it now appears. This (showing another flint) is in a transition state; this (showing another) is a piece of jade, which has been cut on one side and broken on the other. In the case before me I have some of the handiworks of that notorious individual called "Flint Jack." This (holding up a stone) I saw him make, and here are other illustrations. There is no doubt that many of the stones referred to by Dr. Carpenter have been manufactured, and many of the others which you may pick up by thousands in different places, have been produced by the knocking of one against the other. Your Lordship (the Chairman) has just returned from Egypt, where no doubt you found the agates on the plains actually polished as if by the lapidary. Some specimens that have been brought to me by travellers illustrate this in a remarkable degree. The subject would, however, be a long and tedious one to go into, especially after the matter has been so fully discussed on both sides, although, if there were more time, I should be happy to add what I could to what has already been said.

Mr. E. CHARLESWORTH.—I should like to say just a few words upon one point, with regard to the beads, which I think ought not to be altogether overlooked in this discussion. Mr. Whitley held up a string of beads with an air of triumph, and seemed to think he had made a grand hit in catching the advocates of the Palæolithic implements found in the Drift in a great mistake. I do not wish to speak in an irreverent spirit of Mr. Whitley's paper, but it struck me that what he told us was like the production of the play of Hamlet, with Hamlet himself omitted. He intimated that the beads he held up had been regarded as Palæolithic beads. Now, I would ask, who is there among the whole range of men of science who have written on this question, who has said that those beads are Palæolithic beads? Who has ever said that they were the work of Palæolithic man?

Mr. WHITLEY.—Sir Charles Lyell.

Mr. CHARLESWORTH.—I would ask where Sir C. Lyell, Sir John Lubbock, Prestwich, Stevens, or any man of science whose opinion carries the smallest weight, has so stated? Those so-called beads are beads only to the common and vulgar apprehension, and everybody who has at all studied the subject knows that they are fossilized organic bodies, which in many cases do appear to simulate human workmanship. I again assert that no man of science who has ever written on the subject, has ever for a moment put those so-called beads forward as strengthening the theory with regard to the existence of Palæolithic implements. There is one suggestion I would offer, and that is this: like Dr. Carpenter, I am no archæologist, my attention not having been given to the subject. But I went to Norwich, and in the museum of

Mr. Fitch I saw a collection of flint implements from the gravel-bed of the Little Ouse. I said, "Here are certain shapes which to my mind convey the impression that they are of human workmanship, but how far will that impression be modified when I get to the gravel-pits in which the implements were found? Shall I find single specimens myself, or shall I find that there are dozens or scores like these, and so be able to connect the ordinary form of the gravel flints with these flint implements?" I went down to those gravel-beds, and the result was that I did not succeed in meeting with a single specimen of these flint implements, nor did I meet with any form of flint which seemed to connect those in Mr. Fitch's cabinet with the ordinary flints in those pits. Now, if the flints belonging to Mr. Fitch's collection had been produced by accidental fractures, what should I have found? Why, every possible link between those specimens and the ordinary forms of which the gravel-beds were composed.

Mr. WHITLEY.—So you can.

Mr. CHARLESWORTH.—No, there was a wide gap between the two, and I give this as a practical illustration of a fact which every one present can test for himself.

Mr. WHITLEY.—I beg to say that Sir Charles Lyell does state that he thinks it reasonable to assume that these beads formed the necklaces of Palæolithic men. He does not say so in so many words in his text; but he puts it at the head of one of his pages in his book on *The Antiquity of Man.**

Dr. CARPENTER.—Perhaps, as I have paid special attention to this subject, I may be allowed to say one or two words upon it. I have brought with me one of these supposed Palæolithic relics, and it is rather larger than Mr. Whitley's. The "beads," as they are termed, are, no doubt, organized bodies, and there is also no doubt that they grew in this globular form. I apprehend that they grew very often round the stem of a zoophyte, and that this left a natural perforation. Here are some that were picked up by Mr. Prestwich, at Newhaven, and in their case you will see that the natural perforation often does not go through. I do not say that all these perforated beads were artificially bored; I only say that Mr. Whitley has not disproved the probability that some of them were. If you go to any chalk district and pick up a number of these things, you will find that some have a hole right through, while others are merely dimpled. It is of course a curious circumstance, supposing this statement to be true, that only the perforated ones

---

* Sir Charles says, "Granting that there were natural cavities in the axis of some of them, it does not follow that these may not have been taken advantage of for stringing them as beads, while others may have been artificially bored through. Dr. Rigollot's argument in favour of their having been used as necklaces or bracelets, appears to me a sound one. He says he often found small heaps or groups of them in one place, all perforated, just as if, when swept into the river's bed by a flood, the bond which had united them together remained unbroken." (*Antiquity of Man,*" 4th ed., p. 166.) The page is headed, "GLOBULAR SPONGES ARTIFICIALLY PERFORATED."

should have found their way into one place. The idea that these globular bodies were employed as necklace-beads is in a measure justified by the fact stated to me by a gentleman formerly in the Indian medical service, and who has made many valuable researches into the geology of India,—that the inhabitants of Cutch are in the habit of stringing similar things together, and wearing them as necklaces. I do not lay any stress upon this, but at the same time I do not think that Mr. Whitley, by producing three or four specimens of these necklaces made of selected natural beads, has altogether disposed of the matter. For myself I do not think that the beads alone should be taken as evidence of the existence of man at the remote period with which they are identified.

Mr. Evans.—Mr. Whitley has asked whether marks of wear are found on the Palæolithic implements? I reply that the marks of use found on the edges of the flakes and on the edges of the implements discovered in the sand-beds are identical in character with the marks on the flints of a much more recent period, which have evidently been used for scraping hard substances. Mr. Whitley has asked me to point out the sins of which I accused him. They were rather sins of omission than sins of commission. He has cited the beds of Cissbury-hill and Spiennes as containing large numbers of flakes in what he regards as a natural deposit. He ought to know that at those places, pits were found to have been sunk into the chalk for the purpose of obtaining flints to manufacture into flint implements, and that in those pits stag's-horn pickaxes were found—evidence which he ignores. He should have known, too, that implements of a pointed form have been found in Gray's Inn Lane, and that at Hoxne similar implements, regarded as spear-heads, have been discovered. I, myself, bought one at a sale by auction, labelled as a British spear-head, about the human origin of which there could be no question.

Mr. Michell.—At this late hour, I will not detain the meeting long in replying to what has been said. I will only direct attention to the two crucial tests which I have ventured, although, I fear, very feebly, to bring before this meeting. I have spoken of the contrast between the rude chipping, as seen in the Drift types, and that which is seen on the javelin and spear-heads, as shown even on the worst specimens of the Neolithic implements. Taking the Drift flints, you find that the same type prevails throughout, and is as patent in the best specimens in the world as in the roughest I ever picked up. Examining the specimens in the museums, the flints in the beds themselves, and the chipping on shattered flints where the so-called implements are found, I say that the evidence is very strong, and, to my mind, convincingly so, that this chipping on the Drift flints is natural, and not artificial. Compare these again with the specimens belonging to the Second Stone period, where the chipping is undoubtedly artificial, and the contrast is striking. I have asked artisans and flint-knappers, and even "Flint Jack" himself, to make something like this Drift chipping, and they have told me they could not do it. I believe them. Now, I do say that this is something of a test. I ask you to look at the sort of action that takes place where sand is combined with water and both act on the surface of a flint; examine the pieces that are found with no definite form in the sand-beds of Brandon, or wherever you like to go—they may be seen over miles of the Norfolk coast—and I am sure you will say that my view of the chipping is the common-sense view, in the common-sense aspect to which Dr. Carpenter has referred. (Hear, hear.) I have done.

Mr. W. T. CHARLEY, M.P.—I beg to move a vote of thanks to the Earl of Harrowby for his great kindness in presiding this evening. (Cheers.)

The motion having been seconded, and carried unanimously,

The CHAIRMAN said,—In thanking you for the vote you have just passed I must apologize for having come here at all this evening, having no preten-sions, from the previous direction of my studies, to assume such a position; and I should not have assumed it if I had been expected to do more than occupy the chair. Perhaps, however, it may be allowed me, with no pretensions to skill in these matters, to say, so far, that it appears to me to be one of the cases in which antagonism is not quite so real as appears. On the one hand, the very wide range over which these flint-flakes are found, and their enormous numbers, seem to prohibit the conclusion that they are the work of man, and to favour the opposite view, that they must be the result of natural agencies. On the other hand, the forms in which many of them present themselves are so artificial, that it seems impossible not to come to the opposite conclusion. It seems to me to be a question of the analysis of the facts, rather than matters of argument and reasoning, and that such a process is almost im-possible in a meeting like the present. It is certain that there are many cases in which Nature produces results so closely resembling the work of man that it is difficult to draw the line with confidence, and to say, this must be the work of man, and this other may be the work of natural causes. In the valley of the Nile, I have seen instances where flinty substances are in that condition, so placed that apparently they could not have been the work of man, and yet so shaped that it was difficult to see how they could have been the result of natural causes. The action of heat and wind, and water and sand, upon the softer portions of a substance, and with some uniformity, seems to produce results which wonderfully resemble the action of art, and puzzles the observer. I do not see that we are yet able to come to a positive con-clusion on all the facts presented to us.

The proceedings then terminated.

REMARKS.

Rev. S. Lucas, F.G.S.—Notwithstanding the disclaimer of Dr. Carpenter, which I fully accept for himself, and for such distinguished scientists as the late Dr. Buckland, Sir R. I. Murchison, and geologists of their class, there is among many I could name, not only a bias, but what amounts, in appearance at least, to a determination to uphold and push back man's enormous antiquity on most feeble and limited grounds ;* to rest it on a few and often *ques-*

---

* Upon this point, Dr. Dawson, F.R.S. in his work *Acadia*, says— "In a region whose history extends backward scarce three hundred years, prehistoric times may seem to have little interest, in so far as the human period is concerned. Yet I think that something may be learned at a time when prehistoric human remains are exciting so much attention in the old world, by referring to the more recent 'Stone age' of Acadia. Those who speculate as to the antiquity of man, and the ages of Stone, Bronze, and Iron in Europe, and who, looking back on the earlier of these periods through the mists of centuries, attach to it a fabulous antiquity, may derive some lessons from a country in which the Stone age existed three hundred years ago, and has yet passed away as completely as though it had never been. The Micmac still pitches his rude wigwam of birch bark within sight of the largest cities of Acadia ; but he has entered into the Iron age, and the stone weapons of his ancestors are as much objects of curiosity to him as to his neighbours of European origin. * * * * *

"Such was the Stone age of three centuries ago in Acadia ; and it is instructive to bear in mind that in a country in the latitude of France, this was not only the Stone age, but also the age of the caribou or reindeer, and moose and beaver—animals now verging towards extinction, and of no more importance to the present inhabitants than the park deer are to those of the old world. With the exception of a few of the forest-clad, hilly districts, Nova Scotia is now as unsuitable to the existence of the reindeer and moose as France is, and yet three centuries ago these animals were the chief food of its inhabitants. No material change of climate has occurred, but the Iron age has introduced a new race, and the forests have been cleared away. * * * * * *

"The monuments of the Stone age are few. Piles of shells of oysters and other mollusks, in some parts of the coast, mark the site of former summer encampments. Numerous stone implements are found on some old battle-grounds or cemeteries, or on the sites of villages ; and occasional specimens are turned up by the plough. But this is nearly all ; and if the written record of the discovery and colonization of the country did not prevent, we might, in so far as the monumental history is concerned, believe the close of the Stone age to have belonged to a remote antiquity. If the Micmacs had been replaced by a semi-barbarous race, not keeping written records and destroying the aborigines, or incorporating them with themselves, the date of the Stone age would already be altogether uncertain.

"On the whole, nothing can be more striking to any one acquainted with the American Indian, than the entire similarity of the traces of prehistoric man in Europe, to those which remain of the primitive condition of the American aborigines, whether we consider their food, their implements and weapons, or their modes of sepulture ; and it seems evident that if these prehistoric remains are ever to be correctly interpreted by European

tionable facts, and facts which readily admit of being accounted for in harmony with Scripture. I am reminded, however, by the discussion itself that the question is not the broad one of man's antiquity generally, but the *validity* of a branch of the evidence on which that antiquity is sought to be based. Clearly and fully to record my own views on that branch of the evidence, would require an essay. It stands so intimately connected with many other questions, that it can scarcely, with any satisfaction, be discussed separately. I may, without presumption, be permitted to say that my own views on the whole question, which I have long held, and which I have seen no reason to alter, are fully stated in my two last works, *The Biblical Antiquity of Man*, and *The Noaic Deluge*.

With regard to the precise point in dispute, my opinion is, that although vast numbers of the so-called flakes, perhaps *far the greater part* of them, are mere natural productions, yet that many of what are called implements, such, for example, as those exhibited by Mr. J. Evans, and those obtained by Col. Lane Fox, near Acton, are of human origin. But if their *non-artificial* origin could be proved, should we gain anything in the grand dispute itself. The beds from which the implements are obtained have also yielded animal bones—bones of creatures proved to have been contemporary with man—and hence, to disprove the validity of the implements would only remove a part of the evidence of antiquity.* No, the superstructure must embrace a much *wider foundation* than the one brought before the members of the Institute by this discussion. What is meant by the *Drift?* This term is most indefinitely—and, I may add, confusedly—employed by writers and speakers on man's antiquity. Very often it is made to include the *boulder clay*, as well as all of the other overlying deposits, except the most recent ones. The *true Drift* I regard as embracing all the deposits of brick-earth, gravel, and inundation mud—whether in valleys or caves—that are clearly subsequent to the *glacial period.*

These form the human period, whether called Palæolithic or Neolithic, but a period cut into two unequal but prolonged epochs by the Biblical Deluge. And to come to a safe and really philosophical conclusion on this all-im-

— — — —

antiquaries, they must avail themselves of American light for their guidance. Much of this light has already been thrown on this subject by my friend Professor Wilson, in his *Prehistoric Man;* but one can scarcely open any European book on this subject, or glance at any of the numerous articles and papers on this fertile theme in scientific journals, without wishing that those who discuss prehistoric man in Europe, knew a little more of his analogue in America. The subject is a tempting one, but I must close this notice, already too long for the space I should devote to it, by remarking that the relations in America of the short-headed and long-headed races of men, are by no means dissimilar from those of the two similar races in Europe; while it is also evident that some prehistoric skulls, supposed to be of vast antiquity, as, for instance, that of Engis, bear a very close resemblance to those of the Algonquin and Iroquois Indians."—[ED.]

* See note, page 39, No. 3.

(1-8)   e

portant subject, now agitating all thinking minds, the whole evidence of this period must be collected and weighed. To conquer a portion of the field may be useful, but the whole must be conquered before perfect satisfaction can be felt.

S. R. Pattison, Esq., F.G.S.—My opinions agree rather with those of Mr. Evans than those of Mr. Whitley; but having examined the known collections of flint implements, I do not think the facts established by them really militate against Scripture statement or Scripture chronology. True, those who with other views seek to advocate a theory destructive of Biblical chronology, may adduce the facts and assume extended periods, and, the wish being father to the thought, argue for a contradiction. But all the facts of the last mammalian period, in which these evidences of man are discovered, may be synchronized with Scripture. *The annals of Genesis afford time for all the geological and palæontological sequence, so far as the flint tool makers are concerned.*

THE "FLINT IMPLEMENTS IN THE VALLEY OF THE SOMME."

Being a revised and corrected report of a paper recently read by Mr. James Parker, F.G.S., &c.,* before the Ashmolean Society at Oxford.

Mr. Parker said that what he proposed to do was, to point out some of the links in the argument which he thought had not received the attention due to them in comparison with other details introduced into the chain of reasoning, as to the immense antiquity of the flint implements in question. He could not hope, indeed, he did not propose to attempt to explain, the many and varied phenomena presented by the Somme Valley, or to fix the exact age of the beds bearing the flint implements; but he hoped at least to bring forward some considerations which had not been fairly discussed, and which, if founded upon fact, as his observations, he trusted, would show to be the case, militated considerably against the views which were commonly held, and of which Sir Charles Lyell was the chief exponent.† He thought he would best consult the convenience of his audience by giving to them, in Sir Charles Lyell's own words, the chief points in his argument. His work was practically the summing-up of what authors, both English and foreign, had written, together with conclusions derived from his own personal observations. In his book a section of the Valley of the Somme was given. He was sorry to say that as a matter of fact they could place no reliance upon it whatever, as it differed in many respects from the actual circumstances, but it was necessary to reproduce it there in order to illustrate Sir

---

* Mr. Parker has kindly placed this in my hands.—[Ed.]

† Professor Kirk, in his *Age of Man*, p. 23, takes the same view as Mr. Parker.—[Ed.]

Charles Lyell's theories. Quoting from *The Antiquity of Man*, p. 151 (edition of 1873), he read :—

Section across the Valley of the Somme, in Picardy.
(From Lyell's *Antiquity of Man*, 4th ed.)

1. Peat 20 to 30 feet thick resting on gravel, *a*.
2. Lower-level gravel with elephants' bones and flint tools, covered with fluviatile loam, 20 to 40 feet thick.
3. Higher-level gravel, with similar fossils, and with overlying loam, in all 30 feet thick.
4. Upland loam, with shells (*limon de Plateaux*), 5 or 6 feet thick.
5. Eocene tertiary strata, resting on the chalk in patches.

" The chalk hills which bound the valley are almost everywhere between 200 and 300 feet in height. On ascending to that elevation we find ourselves on an extensive table-land, in which there are slight elevations and depressions."

At p. 152,—" Here and there are outlying patches of tertiary sand and clay (bed No. 5), with Eocene fossils, the remnants of a formation, once, more extensive, and which probably once spread in one continuous mass over the chalk, before the present system of valleys had begun to be scooped out,— . . . and their denudation has contributed largely to furnish the materials of gravels in which the flint implements and bones of extinct animals are entombed."

At p. 153,—" The bed marked No. 2 indicates the lower-level gravels, No. 3, the higher ones, or those rising to elevations of 80 or 100 feet above the level of the river. Newer than these is the peat, No. 1, which is from 10 to 30 feet in thickness, and which is not only of later date than the alluvium Nos. 2 and 3, but is also *posterior to the denudation of those gravels, or to the time when the valley was excavated through them*." " Underneath the peat is a bed of gravel from 3 to 14 feet thick, which rests on undisturbed chalk. This gravel was probably formed, in part at least, when the valley was scooped out to its present depth, since which time no geological change has taken place except *the growth of the peat*, and certain oscillations in the general level of the country."

These were briefly the materials for the computation. So many years were ascribed to the peat deposit (this Dr. Lyell placed at 33,000) ; so many in addition for the excavations which had taken place of the valley ; and so many for the deposition of the gravels, marked respectively No. 2 and No. 3. Practically these operations could only be summarized as a whole, and it was only by an induction from a passage elsewhere in his book that they found he computed the time for all these operations somewhere about 70,000 years. At the base, and intermingled with the lowest deposit, were the implements in question.

Although not directly part of the subject before the meeting, he thought it well to say a few words about the 33,000 years of the peat, as it was an important item in the total, and it also afforded a typical instance of the *mode* in which arguments were forced into the service of the author.

He read (p. 156),—" The workmen who cut peat or dredge it from the bottom of swamps and ponds, declare that none of the hollows which they have found or caused by extracting peat have ever been refilled, even to a small extent. *They deny therefore that the peat grows.* This may imply that the increase is not appreciable."

Mr. Parker could only say that on asking a couple of men who were working at M. Tattegrain-Brulé's pit (and who had worked in the peat pit at other times) as to the depth, &c., of the peat, their account distinctly was that it *did* grow. He had not pressed the point at all; the only questions he asked were as to the total depth, and as to what was at the base of the peat. The men agreed that it rested on the chalk, and was nowhere more than nine metres thick. M. Tattegrain-Brulé corrected them so far as to say he knew of places where it was over 30 feet thick, and what was to the present purpose as regarded Sir Charles Lyell's statement, they said that the peat was still growing or forming, and that about a metre in a century was the rate, according to their idea. His own conclusion in 1861 was that this was possibly an average estimate, because when they were altering the moat surrounding Abbeville he observed that there was a deposit of some two or three feet of peat in it, which they were clearing out, and he thought that they would at least have cleared their moat once in a century. This was not far from the Porte Mercadet, a place often referred to in the account of the discoveries.

He might mention the computation which was made for the growth of the peat in Ireland. This was, according to Mr. Griffiths, *two inches* in depth *in one year*; but this was an excessive growth, and under peculiarly favourable circumstances. But before taking such data--the workmen's, which would give at a metre one thousand years for the whole 30 feet, and Mr. Griffiths' computation, which would, under favourable circumstances (and in many places the Somme Valley presents these), leave it possible for the whole 30 feet to have been deposited since the commencement of Queen Anne's reign—he thought it well to call attention to an important consideration which affected materially any computation derived from peat-growth, namely, the intermittent character of the growth—its rapid growth at one time, its slow growth at another, and entire stoppage at others. When the peat, during growth, reached the highest level at which water would stand in any given locality, it naturally ceased to grow. From its character it could not raise itself to any great degree above the element on which it mainly depended for its growth. Of course, it might be in the varied incidents of a long valley that the stream for some cause was kept back, but that could not be for long. The weight of the water would eventually break a course through the obstruction, and then the peat formed at the highest level would sink by reason of evaporation and its own weight, and become more consolidated, and form distinct beds of varied densities, such as existed in the peat, and which pointed to that intermittent character of growth. Consequently, until they knew what periods of rest took place, all computation was impossible, as the facts derived from the observation of incidental growth might have such a relation to the whole as to be not worth taking into account.

Mr. Parker's view was, that only in a very few cases was there any material growth of peat, such as when the water stood sufficiently above its surface as to supply the means of growth; and that then it was very rapid, the conditions being as favourable as those in Ireland; and it followed, therefore, that as the peat grew higher in the valley—higher, that is to say, in regard to the sea-level—so, fewer occasions would there be of the water lying at a sufficiently high level to induce growth; and from this the probabilities were that in the earlier history of the peat, the occasions being more frequent, the beds would increase as a whole far more rapidly than they did now.

He next turned to Sir Charles Lyell's computation. This writer had selected the argument from M. Boucher de Perthes' evidence, and though he said "we must hesitate before adopting it," he gave it as the only one of any value, and did not intimate the least wherein any fallacy lay. It was given at p. 156.

" In one case, however, M. Boucher de Perthes observed several flat dishes of Roman pottery, lying in a horizontal position in the peat, the shape of which must have prevented them from sinking into or penetrating through the underlying peat. Allowing about fourteen centuries for the growth of the superincumbent vegetable matter, he calculated that the thickness gained in a hundred years would be no more than *three French centimetres*. This rate of increase (Sir Charles Lyell added) would demand *so many tens of thousands of years* for the formation of the entire thickness of 30 feet, that we must hesitate before adopting it as a chronometric scale."

It was obvious that 0·03 metres in a century required upwards of 33,000 years to give the 10 metres, which in some places existed in the Somme Valley. The point he would lay stress upon was, that the hesitation to accept this should not have been made to arise from the result which it gave, but from the fact that the data were so obviously worthless for forming any calculation at all. The absolute but erroneous assumption that continual formation of peat went on at one uniform rate, was the basis of the whole argument. This pottery was found, so it was stated in M. Boucher de Perthes' book (*Antiquités Celtiques*, ii. p. 135), to be 0·60 metres (nearly 2 feet) below the surface. This writer argued further that much of the peat being impure, the factor had to be reduced to one-fourth, *i.e.*, to 0·45. Now, Samian pottery, it was argued, must be 1,400 or 1,500 years old. It was assumed (*a*) that at that distance of time it was (*b*) placed gently on the surface of the turbary so as not to sink through, and (*c*) circumstances were such that it was not buoyed up, and (*d*) that the peat from that moment down to 1863, had gradually, and at one uniform rate per annum, grown over it. Any one of the conditions of course being liable seriously to affect the factor, they were supposed to accept all, and thereby obtain a factor to apply generally to the growth of the peat throughout the Somme Valley. If this was not what was meant by Sir Charles Lyell's argument, nothing could be gleaned from it at all. The lecturer then proceeded to consider the next elements for the computation of the time which had elapsed since the deposition of the implement-bearing beds. Without quoting new passages, the words already given showed the line of argument, namely, " that the peat was posterior to the time when the valley was excavated through the gravels."

It was in vain to look for any figures of computation for such excavation, although elsewhere in Sir Charles Lyell's book (p. 367) it was intimated that the upper and earliest of these gravels were the equivalents probably of beds 100,000 years old, no arguments were forthcoming as to the means of computation. Indeed, it seemed beyond all calculation. Imagine the rate at which a trickling stream could excavate and grow into a large one, and carry down the material of a valley 115 miles long, and varying from one mile to ten miles broad. Imagine the millions upon millions of tons of chalk and of other material to be scooped out and carried along and deposited in the sea. The time was certainly beyond all calculation, and the 67,000 years, he was sure, would be found by any one who considered the problem carefully to represent but a mere unit in the time required under the circumstances.

But then the question forced itself on one, " Was the Somme Valley excavated by the Somme River at all ?" Not one line would be found in evidence ; it was assumed purely and absolutely, and on that assumption alone were based all the arguments as to time, which were put forward.

In considering the hypothesis of the excavation of a valley of this kind by means of a river, the first question to be asked was naturally, " Where did the water come from ?" Considering the vast surface to be removed, it was necessary to have a supply of water of enormous quantity and of constant flow. And much more than that, it was necessary to have an impetus given to that water by a fall or gathering together of streams to give it force sufficient to remove, and propel the loosened material forward in its downward progress to the sea.

Two minor considerations also might be mentioned which in a full investigation of the phenomena should not be overlooked, though the scope of the present argument would not allow of any further remarks upon them. First, a certain amount of slope of the bed of the valley from its highest to its lowest point must be necessary, for below a certain incline water would not move large masses forward to any extent. Now, the bed of the Somme valley was singularly level for a wide river, there being a fall of little more than 200 feet from the the source of the Somme to the sea, a distance of 115 miles; in fact, the fall was hardly above that of the Thames between Oxford and London, and the distance was the same. Second, there was the consideration of the difficulty of accounting for the disposal of the materials when they reached the river's mouth. He had examined very carefully the district at the mouth of the Somme, and could say that they were not deposited there, nor were there any signs of them. Nor yet was any *à priori* ground for arguing that the waves had washed the *débris* into their depths. The history of the coast was directly opposed to this, as the waves were throwing up sand-dunes, and had been so since the earliest times of which they had any record regarding that coast.

Mr. Parker then referred to a large diagram which he had prepared, and on which he had traced the main line of the Somme, with its several arteries —representing by broad lines of colour the several valleys converging into the main valley. The district represented on the diagram was about 140 miles from east to west, and about 60 miles from north to south. At the eastern end it would be observed that the Somme was simply a small stream, scarcely to be called a river in a strict sense. Of course, it was in a way the river Somme, because they considered the source of a river to be the point of departure of the farthest of the numerous streams which go to make up that river, and in most cases it was little more than water trickling along a ditch from some spring. But the word river in its natural sense means the stream of water after many smaller streams had been combined together, and had contributed each one its quota to form the larger one. The history of nearly all rivers was this, and the Somme was no exception. It depended on the drainage of many sloping valleys converging into the main valley. At the upper part it was a brook, and it did not become a river properly so called, till it had received the converging rivulets of many small valleys. Till then it was no river; it had no force whatever. It was necessary for the converging valleys to be there to supply the water; it was necessary for the valley to exist to supply the fall; so that when they were asked to accept that the river Somme made the valley of the Somme, it seemed to him they were asked to believe that the river made the conditions by which itself was called into existence.

It was unreasonable, on the other hand, to imagine high hills, pouring forth a stream of water above S. Quentin. They could not have existed without so total a subversion of the levels of the country, that there would be no need of calling in the aid of river action to account for valleys twice as great as the Somme valley. But as a matter of fact, geologically, such lofty hills could not have existed without leaving a trace behind them.

Looking at the great system of arteries shown in the diagram, the ground to the south-east was *on an average* higher than that to the north-west. There were here and there hills of the same height, or almost the same, along the whole line, and they were broken up by innumerable valleys and "combes"; but by taking the average from a considerable number it would be seen that there was a general slope, as regards the higher prominence, in a north-westerly direction. The hill rising immediately above the source of the Somme, five miles N.E. of S. Quentin, and at a place called from the circumstance " Fon-somme," only reached 308 feet in height above the level of the sea, and the drainage of this alone supplied the upper tributary. Three miles to the south-east was a hill reaching 400 feet ; but it appeared to add little, if anything, to the supply. They would have to go several miles to obtain a higher level, and directly they reached it they found that it no longer supplied the Somme ; but the Aisne and the Oise, which were tributaries of the Seine, and belonged to a distinct system. If they continued their search for still loftier elevations, they would, still proceeding in a south-easterly direction, find hills rising to 800 and 900 feet ; but they gave off their streams to tributaries of the Meuse, and they would be obliged to follow their waters through Holland before they were discharged into the sea. In a word, the whole system depended upon the water-sheds of the hills rising only to 300 and 400 feet above the level of the sea. The Somme depended mainly for its water upon the combined supplies of its chief tributaries, the Avre, the Noye, and the Celle ; but all along its course it was assisted by numerous smaller streams gathering the rain-water which fell upon the slopes of the numerous ravines descending into the main valley.

But connected with the Somme system, it was pointed out that there were several parallel rivers following the same course as the Somme, i.e., descending from the south-eastern ridge in a north-westerly direction. To the north the Authie, and to the south the Bresle, the Yeres, the Eaulne, and the Bethune. They depended also upon the same sources of water, and were in every respect similar in their circumstances, and could scarcely have been different in their origin. If it were objected that springs now no longer in existence might have originally supplied a much larger body and a much greater force of water than now, it must be remembered that the district was a chalk district. Each ravine was as a rule dependent upon the rainfall of its own slope. All that could be done, therefore, was to increase the rainfall, and add, what perhaps there might be independent reason for adding, heavy snowfalls, and of long duration, by which the April suns provided an amount of water far in excess of what was thrown down the ravine now. And yet that would affect the argument but little, because the sloping ravines converging to the great general valley must have been already there before the excessive rainfall or snowfall could be of any value. The sudden melting of snows on large flat expanses produced no material results ; it was the valley, the ravine, and the gully which gave the force to the water, and without them the water but evaporated into the atmosphere or soaked away as best it might.

It was not a part of his task then to explain the phenomena of the Somme valley ; but with that map before him he felt called on to say a few words as to the operations which he thought it suggested. He might add that the view he took was based not only on the data then before them, but upon the study of the levels of the Ordnance Survey in a much more minute degree than was represented by the figures on his diagram, and beyond this by many a tramp over the hills in question, sometimes in geological excursions, more often archæological. The great parallel lines of rivers, the furrows as it were stretching in a direction similar to that of the sloping chalk, suggested that the river valleys belonged to the operations consequent on the upheaval of the great mass of chalk from its ocean bed. He compared the result with what any one might see on any argillaceous shore, where the base was impervious and yet soft. The descending tide left channels and furrows, by which the surface was drained, but afterwards modified in character by evaporation and exposure to atmospheric influence. The great chalk expanse of a hundred miles was enormous in comparison to the few yards of a tidal shore, and so were the valleys of 100 and 200 feet depth to the little drifts of two or three inches. But this was not all. If it were argued that the effect was not proportionately sufficient, it might also be reasonably replied that the emergence of this vast chalk-bed from the ocean was probably not of that passive character which belonged to a tide receding from the shore ; but, it might well have been the result of active elevation of the chalk, and such elevation could scarcely have been unaccompanied by fissures and inequalities which, as a rule, would lie, as regards their greater intensity, in lines at right angles to the main axis of elevation. That was just what those valleys did, and the minor fissures represented by the smaller ravines lay again in a general sense at right angles to them, as might be seen by a glance at the Ordnance map before them, on which the valleys were slightly tinted. The general aspect of the Somme valley and its tributary ravines pointed distinctly to operations connected with the rising from the ocean bed. Whether that took place in tertiary or post-tertiary times, whether once or more than once, were not questions with which he had now to deal. All he would lay stress on was that those rivers and valleys, and among them the Somme river and Somme valley, did not owe their origin to the slow excavation of river action, and therefore the assumption of that action, as a measure of time in connection with phenomena which the valley presented, was an absolute error.

He next passed on to the consideration of the deposition of the gravels. Practically the two arguments were based upon the same premise. The current of the Somme excavated the valley, and in doing so deposited the upper-level gravel. It afterwards excavated the upper-level gravel, and deposited the lower-level gravel. It afterwards excavated that gravel, and the 33,000 years of the peat-formation set in. At least, this was what was meant if there was any meaning in Sir Charles Lyell's argument at all. It was difficult to quote one single passage stating this. At p. 168 there was a good deal about beds 1, 2, and 3 ; but it would be found that the reference was to another set of beds in another section and in reverse order. And yet the descriptions were intended to be a continuation of the same argument. Again at p. 173, in referring to the first section for comparison with the Menchecourt beds, he spoke of No. 2 as the lower-level gravel, and No. 3 as higher alluvium ; but at p. 169 the low-level beds at Menchecourt were spoken of as the older alluvium. He could not but think that if a clearer explanation of the phenomena had been given, the fallacies involved in the conclusions would have presented themselves to the mind of the readers if not to that of the compiler of the book.

Before quitting this part of the subject, Mr. Parker referred to the passage at p. 186, where it was said there were " patches of drift at heights intermediate between the higher and lower gravel, and also some deposits showing that the river once flowed at elevations above as well as below the level of the platform of St. Acheul." He pointed out how practically the line of demarcation between high and low level gravels did not exist in fact, and that the argument therefore in regard to age derived from this difference of level was wholly untenable.

Having treated of the general aspect of the Somme valley as regarded the evidence for the antiquity of the implement-bearing beds, he gave an account of the position of the beds in a particular district, namely, that of S. Acheul, about 1½ mile east of Amiens, a district said to have yielded more of the flint implements in a small space than any other.

The plan exhibited some ten or twelve pits or cuttings in a space of about one mile from east to west, and three-quarters of a mile north to south. The levels of the surface of pits were marked, and a series of coloured sections of the sides of the pits, &c., drawn to scale. From these it appeared that while there was a gentle slope of the surface of the ground towards the south, there was a very rapid descent of the underlying chalk in a particular part, and in this hollow there had been the accumulation which contained the flint implements. The actual section presented a " combe " in the chalk filled up nearly to the level of the sides with gravels and sands, not stratified horizontally, which would have been the case had they been the result of deposit in a wide expanse of river, nor following any line suggested by possible current action.

He pointed out also in several instances, that in a general sense the gravels were dependent on the chalk contours, but presented also the kind of inequalities which would arise from subaërial action. The surface materials seemed to have fallen, slipped, or drifted into lower levels, and arranged themselves partly according to their relative gravities, partly, as said before, according to the ground on which they fell or over which they passed. And finally the varied action of wind drifting the surface sand and loam, of rain washing and separating lighter materials, and the possibly far more effective action of the melting snows, in loosening, shifting, and undermining the previously formed gravel—all those causes, coupled with the fact that they were no doubt intermittent, and acting only at perhaps long and irregular intervals, were necessary to be taken into account in understanding the various phenomena which were seen in the details of the sections. Neither, then, in the consideration of the general phenomena, nor in the minute details were there any circumstances which suggested river action ; on the contrary, they militated against it, and suggested subaërial action. But this being so, the very basis of Sir Charles Lyell's computation of enormous time was cut away. It was made to depend upon the slow action of the river cutting through an enormous chalk plateau, and carrying down to the sea millions of tons of chalk and other material, and all this before a peat formation commenced, which took 33,000 years. It was not his object to argue how long those beds might have been in formation under subaërial action, or how short a time was sufficient ; the many accidents arising from the combination of the varied circumstances already detailed, rendered all argument as to measure of time very uncertain ; but what his object had been was to show that the computation put forth by Sir Charles Lyell, and followed by so many others, was based upon utterly false premises.

Mr. Parker, before concluding, drew attention to a large collection of flint implements derived from the St. Acheul beds, chiefly from his own cabinet, but supplemented by others, by S. Sharp, Esq., F.G.S. Also implements from other places, and from bone caves, turbaries, British burial-mounds, &c., &c., for the sake of comparison.

He pointed out that if rudeness was a criterion of immense antiquity, several of those from the British graves at Brighthampton, near Oxford, found with characteristic British pottery, must be put long anterior in date to the St. Acheul implements, which were of a more developed type ; in fact, the very perfection of the St. Acheul implements, while it told, on the one hand, with overwhelming force in favour of their being the work of man, at the same time militated against the enormous antiquity ascribed to them, unless we imagined man to have been wholly stationary, if not even retrogressive in the art of fabrication of his necessary implements of domestic and aggressive life.

The President (Professor Rollestone) said that as every part of the world was now shown to have had a flint period, it bore on the interesting anthropological question whether man rose from a savage state, or whether the present savage was a degradation from a higher state.

PRIMITIVE MAN AND REVELATION.*

By Principal J. W. Dawson, LL.D., F.R.S., M'Gill College, Montreal.
Hon. For. Correspondent of the Victoria Institute.

The battle-ground of opposition in the name of Science and Philosophy to the Holy Scriptures is ever changing, but in modern times most of it, in so far as Science is concerned, has centred on the early history of the earth and man as contained in Genesis. One portion of the controversy may be held to be disposed of. The geological record is so manifestly in accordance with the Mosaic history of creation that to all those (unfortunately as yet too few) who have an adequate knowledge of both stories, the anticipation of our modern knowledge of Astronomy, Physics, and Geology in the early chapters of Genesis is so marked as to constitute a positive proof of inspiration. Recent discoveries and hypotheses have given another turn to the discussion, and have directed it to questions relating to primitive man and the connection of the modern period with previous geological eras. Man, we are told, is a descendant of inferior animals. His primitive condition was one of half brutal barbarism. His rise to the actual position of humanity was through countless ages of progressive development, extending over periods vastly longer than those of Sacred history. These doctrines, supported by much plausible show of proof, are given forth by popular writers as ascertained results of scientific research, and we are asked to accept a new Genesis, shorn of all the higher spiritual features of that with which we are familiar, holding forth no idea of individual life and salvation, but only a dim prospect of some elevation of the race as the result of an indefinite struggle for existence in the future.

Many good men are naturally anxious as to whereto this may grow, and whether we are not on the brink of a decided breach between the Word of God and the study of the earliest human remains. My own belief is that the doctrines of the antiquity and descent of man, as held by the more extreme evolutionists, have attained to their maximum degree of importance, and that henceforth the more advanced speculators must retrace their steps toward the old beliefs, leaving, however, some most valuable facts in explanation of the early history of man. The subject is too extensive to allow of a full exposition of my reasons for this belief in the time to which this address must be limited, but I may refer to a few of the most recent facts in proof of my statement.

The physical characters of the known specimens of primitive men are unfavourable to the doctrine of evolution. Theories of derivation would lead us to regard the most degraded races of men as those nearest akin to the primitive stock ; and the oldest remains of man should present decided approximation to his simian ancestors. But the fact is quite otherwise. With the exception of the celebrated Neanderthal skull, which stands alone, and is of altogether unascertained date, the skulls of the most ancient European men known to us, are comparable with those of existing races, and further,

---

* The value of Dr. Dawson's paper will be apparent to all who have watched the controversy, of which the Flint Implement discussion is one phase ; it was read at the New York Conference last year, and he has now kindly placed a revised and corrected copy in my hands.—[Ed.]

the great stature and grand development of the limbs in those of the most ancient skeletons which are entire or nearly so, testify to a race of men more finely constituted physically than the majority of existing Europeans. The skull found by Schmerling in the Cave of Engis, associated with the bones of the mammoth and other extinct animals, is of good form and large capacity, and presents characters which, though recalling those of some European races, also resemble those of the native races of America. The bones described by Christy and Lartet from the Cave of Cro-Magnon, in France, represent a race of great stature, strength, and agility, and with a development of brain above the European average ; but the lines of the face show a tendency to the Mongolian and American visage, and the skeletons present peculiarities in the bones of the limbs found also in American races, and indicating, probably, addiction to hunting and a migratory and active life. These Cro-Magnon people lived at an epoch when France was overgrown with dense forests, when the mammoth probably lingered in its higher districts, and when a large part of the food of its people was furnished by the reindeer. Still more remarkable, perhaps, is the fossil man, as he has been called, of Mentone, recently found in a cave in the South of France, buried under cavern accumulations which bespeak a great antiquity, and associated with bones of extinct mammalia and with rudely-fashioned implements of flint. It appears from the careful descriptions of Dr. Rivière that this man must have been six feet high and of vast muscular power, more especially in the legs, which present the same American peculiarities already referred to in the Cro-Magnon skeletons. The skull is of great capacity, the forehead full, and the face, though broad and Mongolian and large-boned, is not prognathous, and has a high facial angle. The perfect condition of the teeth, along with their being worn perfectly flat on the crowns, would imply a healthy and vigorous constitution and great longevity, with ample supplies of food, probably vegetable, while the fact that the left arm had been broken and the bone healed shows active and possibly warlike habits. Such a man, if he were to rise up again among us, might perhaps be a savage, but a noble savage, with all our capacity for culture, and presenting no more affinity to apes than we do.

If the question be asked, What precise relation do these primitive European men bear to anything in sacred history ? we can only say that they all seem to indicate one race, and this allied to the old Turanian stock of Northern Asia, which has its outlying branches to this day both in America and Europe. If they are antediluvians, they show that the old Nephelim and Gibborim of the times before the flood were men of great physical as well as mental power, but not markedly distinct from modern races of men. If they are postdiluvians, then they reveal the qualities of the old Rephaim and Anakim of Palestine, who not improbably were of Turanian stock. In any case, they may well have points of historical contact with the Bible, if we were better informed as to their date and distribution.

I have referred to European facts only, but it is remarkable that in America the oldest race known to us is that of the ancient Alleghans and Toltecans and their allies, and that these, too, were men of large stature and great cranial development, and agricultural and semi-civilized, their actual position being not dissimilar from that attributed to the earliest cultivators of the soil in the times of Adam or Noah.

So far the facts bearing on the physical and mental condition of primitive man are not favourable to evolution, and are more in accordance with the theory of Divine Creation, and with the statements of the sacred record.

Recent facts with reference to primitive man show that his religious beliefs were similar to those referred to in Scripture. The whole of the long isolated tribes of America held to a primitive monotheism or belief in a Great Spirit, who was not only the creator and ruler of the heaven and the earth, but had the control of countless inferior spirits—manitous or ministering angels. They also believed in an immortality and a judgment of all men beyond the grave. Hence arose in various forms the doctrine of guardian manitous, represented by tokens or teraphim, and watching over individuals, families, and places. Hence arose also the practice of burying with the dead the things he had valued in life, as likely, in the vague imaginings of the untaught mind, to be useful in the other world. Their traditions also embraced in various and crude forms the idea of a mediator or intercessor between God and man. No one who studies these beliefs of the American tribes can fail to recognize in them the remnants of the same primitive theology which we have in the patriarchal age of the Bible, and more or less in the religions of all ancient peoples of whom we have historical records. I may say here in passing that the tenacity with which the red man of America has clung in his barbarism and long isolation, to remnants of primitive truth, is an additional reason why we should strive to give him a purer gospel.

With reference to those prehistoric men, known to us only by their bones and implements, it may not be possible to discover their belief as to the unity of God; but we have distinct evidence on the other points. On the oldest bone implements—some of them made of the ivory of the now extinct mammoth—we find engraved the totems or manitou-marks of their owners, and in some cases scratches or punctures, indicating the offerings made or successes and deliverances experienced under their auspices. With regard to the belief in immortality, perhaps also in a resurrection, the Mentone man — whose burial is perhaps the oldest known to us—was interred with his fur robes and his hair dressed as in life, with his ornaments of shell wampum on his head and limbs, and with a little deposit of oxide of iron, wherewith to paint and decorate himself with his appropriate emblems. Nor is he alone in this matter. Similar provision for the dead appears at Cro-Magnon and the Cave of Bruniquel. Thus the earliest so-called Palæolithic men entertained beliefs in God and in immortality, perhaps the dim remains of primitive theism, perhaps the result of their perception of the invisible things of God in the works that He had made.

The antiquity of man as revealed by his prehistoric remains has probably been greatly exaggerated. A careful study of the latest edition of *The Antiquity of Man*, by Sir C. Lyell, in which that great geologist has summed up all the scattered evidence on this point, must leave this impression. The particular facts adduced are individually doubtful and susceptible of different interpretations, though collectively they present an imposing appearance, and many of them have been weakened by recent observations and discoveries. American analogies teach us, as I propose to show in papers soon to be published, that undue importance has been attached to the distinctions of Neolithic and Palæolithic ages. The physical changes which have taken place since the advent of man have been measured by standards inapplicable to them, and the extinct quadrupeds of the later post-Pliocene period may have lived nearer to our time than has been supposed. No human remains have been found in beds older than the close of the so-called Glacial period, and the earlier indications succeeding this period are not actual bones of men. but only rude implements, some of which are possibly naturally-shaped stones, and others have had their antiquity exaggerated by misapprehension as to the mode of their occurrence.

It is, however, probable that the investigations now in progress will establish the fact that, in the earlier part of man's residence in the Old Continent, he was contemporary with many great quadrupeds now extinct, and that some of them, as well as some races of men, may have perished in a great continental subsidence which occurred early in the modern or human period. Both of these conclusions will, I think, bring themselves finally into harmony with the Biblical account of the antediluvian world, notwithstanding the strenuous opposition of the large party opposed to any correlation of natural and spiritual truth.

Science may soon enable us to account for the divergence of mankind into permanent races in a way more satisfactory than heretofore. It has heretofore been a stumbling-block with many in the doctrine of the unity of man, that we find evidence of distinctness of race as great as at present in early Egyptian monuments. Modern ideas of derivation have swept away this as an infidel objection, but they have not failed to demand an enormous lapse of time for the early development of these races. A new law is, however, coming into view, which may render this unnecessary. It is that species, when first introduced, have an innate power of expansion, which enables them rapidly to extend themselves to the limits of their geographical range, and also to reach the limits of their divergence into races. These limits once reached, the races run on in parallel lines until they one by one run out and disappear. According to this law, the most aberrant races of men might be developed in a few centuries, after which divergence would cease, and the several lines of variation would remain permanent, at least so long as the conditions under which they originated remained. This new law, which was hinted at long ago by Hall, the Palæontologist of New York, is coming more distinctly into view, and will probably altogether remove one of the imagined necessities of a great antiquity of man. It may prove also to be applicable to language as well as to physical characters.

I have given above only a few examples out of many which may be adduced that the results of natural science as applied to man, however they may at first seem to conflict with the truth of God, will ultimately come into harmony with it.

One object in referring to these subjects here has been to invite the attention of Christians to certain errors in the treatment of such subjects, which I observe to be prevalent, and which I think every Christian man of science must sincerely deprecate.

The first is the hasty reception of broad popular statements of leading scientists as if they were received and proved conclusions. Nearly every new scientific fact and principle is at first only imperfectly understood and partially misapplied, and statements much too unguarded are often made by enthusiastic votaries of particular specialties.

The second is the resting content with the shallow assertion that the Bible need not be in harmony with Nature. The Bible is not a text-book of Science, nor are spiritual truths always directly reconcilable at first with natural truths. But the Bible, as a Book of God, cannot outrage Nature, and there are necessary harmonies between the natural and the spiritual. Weak admissions that the Bible accommodates itself to errors as to Nature may save the theologian tho trouble of inquiry, and may be welcomed by men of science as setting them free from dogmatic trammels; but the earnest votary of science who is not a Christian despises those who make them, and regards their doctrine as worthless.

A third is the connection of ancient superstitions or modern ecclesiastical expediencies with God's Word. Science is in its nature hostile to superstition, and to hypocritical expediency   *   *   I believe that much of the antagonism of men of science is really excited by accessions which are not of God, but the growth of human device in darker ages of the world. I would not ask the Christian to accommodate his creed to any requirements of the science or literature of our day. That would be an equally fatal error. What I ask is that the scriptural truth may be presented unmixed with extraneous matters, not of the Bible, but of man.

Lastly, the Christian must not despise as unworthy of attention the current scientific doctrines on such subjects. If the missionary thinks it necessary to study the beliefs of the rudest tribes, that he may better teach them the truth, surely we must not ignore the latest results of the intellectual work of the most cultivated men, which in any case is sure to influence the mind of the time, and which, properly treated, must yield positive results for the cause of God.

The scientific infidel is not always a wrong-doer to be put down. He is often a very darkened soul, struggling for light, and sometimes driven back from it by the follies and inconsistencies of Christians. The lamentable and growing separation between those who study God's works and those who believe in His word is not all of it the fault of the scientist. The theologian will be held responsible for so much of it as may result from his adulterating the water of life with unwholesome earthly elements.

www.ingramcontent.com/pod-product-compliance
Lightning Source LLC
Chambersburg PA
CBHW022030080426
42733CB00007B/784